The New Paint along with NANCY KOMINSKY

Oil painting made easy

by Nancy Kominsky

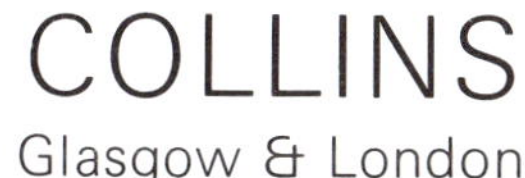

COLLINS

Glasgow & London

First published 1975
Second impression 1976
Published by William Collins Sons & Co. Ltd, Glasgow and London

Designed and edited by Youé and Spooner Ltd

© Sportontv 1975
Filmset by Tradespools Limited, Frome, Somerset
Printed in Great Britain
ISBN 0 00 411832 4

For all the paintings in this book Nancy Kominsky has used Rowney Georgian Oil Colours which she has found to be the most suitable for her purposes. They are permanent and their consistency is incomparable for palette knife painting.

Contents

Introduction

When the first *Paint Along with Nancy Kominsky* book and television series was launched, I realised old ideas die hard, especially where art is concerned and specifically the art of painting.

First and foremost, there are many who are still convinced that the ability to draw and paint is something you are born with – like blue eyes – and that it cannot be taught. They harbour the wild and romantic notion that, on a frenzy of inspiration, one rushes to the canvas (meanwhile a little elf has prepared the palette, canvas, etc) and creates a masterpiece. Forget it – it just isn't so. Through my teaching over the years of hundreds of happy and productive students from all over the world, I have proved that, with my simplified method, anyone, regardless of how puny his talent, can learn to paint.

In painting, colour is even more important than the drawing and, incidentally, the most frustrating aspect for the beginner – hence the colour formulas in exact amounts (just like recipes), which take the guesswork out of painting. By following this method, you can learn to draw and paint at the same time. Even Delacroix believed that 'colour, not draughtsmanship, is the basis of painting'.

When you begin to paint, the key is to keep your paintings simple, and one of the best ways of achieving successful results is by copying other subjects. Original works should be attempted only after you have mastered the simple mechanics of painting (i.e. colour, compositions, etc). The word 'copy' always creates screams of protest and horror from the purists, but the beginner can court disaster because he does not know how to be discriminating in his choice of subject. In order to become familiar with painting procedures and colour formulas, copy from the carefully chosen subjects in this book. As a matter of fact, Manet, Degas (who copied in Italy for years from the old masters and evolved his own style) and Toulouse-Lautrec used photographs for reference for their paintings, and the best work of Utrillo was done from picture postcards. Copying doesn't necessarily mean you imitate the artist's style, for no two painters see things in exactly the same way.

So follow carefully the recipes for the colour formulas, the stroke-by-stroke methodical instructions for each painting in this book, and I promise you will be thrilled with every attempt you make.

Painting materials

The following colours and other required painting materials, which are illustrated on page 9, can be purchased under the Nancy Kominsky label. However, you can buy them separately, if you wish, from most art material stockists.

No substitutions of colours should be made, otherwise your colour mixes will not turn out the same as those in this book.

PAINTS

Lemon Yellow
Yellow Ochre
Naples Yellow
Cadmium Yellow deep
Cadmium Orange
Vermilion (red)
Alizarin Crimson
Viridian (green)
French Ultramarine (blue)
Burnt Umber
Extra large tube of Zinc or Flake White

PALETTE KNIVES

Offset knife, for painting
Straight knife, for mixing colour (optional)

BRUSHES

1 large, flat hog brush, for umber wash
1 medium round brush, for drawing

OTHER MATERIALS

Easel — whatever available and sturdy. A table easel is very useful if you are short of space as, not only does it fold away, but the table on which you place it then provides a good surface on which to put all your painting supplies.

Turpentine, or white spirit if you do not like the smell of turpentine. (This is the medium for cleaning your brushes.)

Large square wooden palette or tear-off palette pad.

Single tin dipper for the medium of turpentine or white spirit.

Canvas or canvas boards, 14 in. (36cm) by 18 in. (46cm). If you do not want the expense of either of these, use hardboard which is adequate. Go to a timber yard and have a large piece cut into 14 in. (36cm) by 18 in. (46cm) sizes. Paint each piece with cheap white undercoat on either the rough or smooth side (depending on your preference) and leave them to dry thoroughly before use.

Toilet tissue which is disposable and therefore more practical and cleaner than cloths.

Plastic litter bag.

Polythene or tin foil. Use either of these to cover your left-over paint on the palette, pop it in the fridge and your paint will keep indefinitely.

Artists' clear picture varnish. There is no hurry for this, as paintings should not be varnished in under six months' drying time.

WORK AREA

The ideal would be a room facing north but you will probably end up in a corner of any room that is spare, using electric light. It is really unimportant where you work, as long as you have the space to move and are comfortable. After all, Michelangelo painted on his back with a candle strapped to his head for four years and you cannot do better than the Sistine Chapel!

Measurements for colour formulas

In a painting colour is most important — even more than the drawing. At the risk of sounding unartistic and homey, I have broken down colour into almost exact amounts, rather like a recipe. I am going to use spoons for measuring, as this helps to keep amounts uniform. Of course, this gives me qualms, as I have visions of paint actually being measured out with spoons. Don't. Just gauge it by eye. This naturally means the amounts are not level.

The illustration below shows the amounts used in colour mixtures.

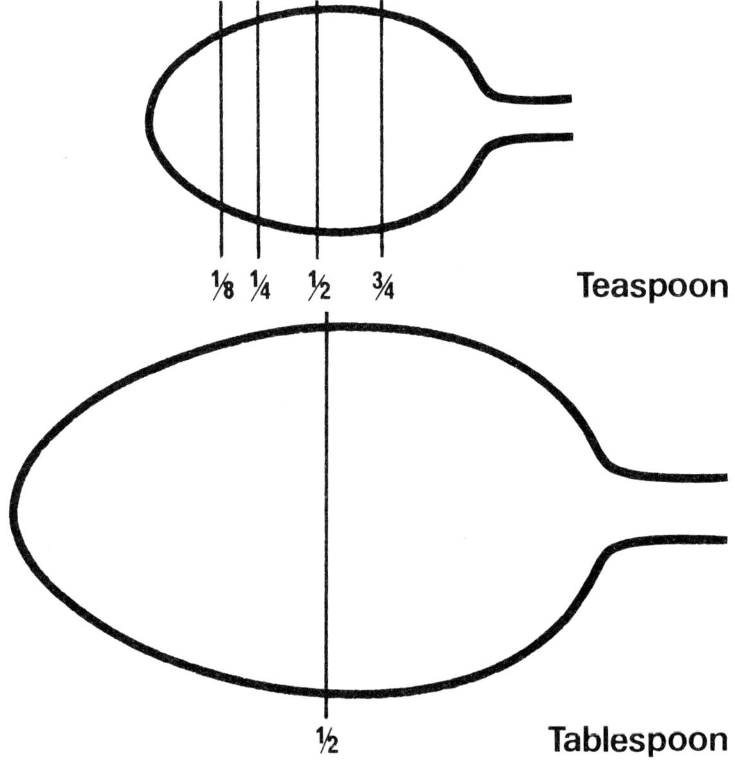

These amounts are geared mostly for knife painting which requires more paint, and ensure having the adequate amount of paint for each area in the painting. (You can use just as much paint by mixing in bits and dabs, which is both a nuisance and time-consuming.)

Keep your piles of mixed paint clean. If you have any mixed paint left over when you have finished a painting, remove the separate piles from the mixing area and arrange them in a neat line alongside the squeezed-out paints on the palette. Clean the mixing area, then cover the palette with polythene or tin foil and put it in the fridge or a cool, dark place. You can use left-over paint to work on a smaller canvas another time.

The colour formulas in this series can be used for other paintings as well. For instance, if you see a photograph or painting of a landscape that you would like to copy, use the colour formulas for Bonnie Banks (on page 21) or Early Spring (on page 47). Use a fairly good-sized photograph (for example from a calendar), or postcards, or even copy from the Impressionists such as Monet and Van Gogh. Cover the photograph or painting with a sheet of polythene, then, with a medium round brush and umber wash, draw in the grid lines and the picture, on the polythene, as shown in the drawings in this book. You can then transfer your drawing correctly on to canvas.

However, before you embark on this sort of experiment, finish the carefully chosen subjects in this book. In this way, you will feel more confident and courageous.

Painting procedures

1 Your first step is to cover the canvas with an umber wash. This gives the painting a richer colour and also allows you to wipe off the drawing if you make a mistake. To make the umber wash, squeeze out $\frac{1}{2}$ teaspoon burnt umber. Dip your large, flat hog brush into the turpentine or white spirit (it should not be dripping), and then into the burnt umber on the palette, pulling some aside to make a light, rather thin wash. Cover the canvas with the wash, taking care not to make it too dark or runny. Wipe the excess moisture with tissue but leave the canvas damp.

2 For the sectioning on the canvas use the medium round brush and umber wash. This time, use more burnt umber than turpentine or white spirit, in order to achieve a darker colour. If your canvas is to be used vertically, draw three vertical lines equally spaced and five horizontal lines. If your canvas is to be used horizontally, section it off with five equally spaced vertical lines and three horizontal lines (see the vertical drawing on page 12 and the horizontal drawing on page 24).

3 Put in the drawing reduced to simple form and the shading with the same dark umber wash and the medium round brush. Use tissue to erase, if necessary.

4 Set up your palette as shown in the photograph and key illustration on the following pages, using about a teaspoonful of each colour and mixing the aqua, purple and mixed green as instructed. The palette should be set up the same way each time and a copy of the set-up kept for reference.

5 Be accurate when mixing your colours. You may find that your colour mixtures vary slightly from the colour swatches shown in the book but this is normal. Just make sure that you keep the correct tonal values.

6 Keep your paint on your palette clean while working, by cleaning your knife before going from one colour to another.

7 Dabbling and stippling are two techniques you will find used in this book. To stipple

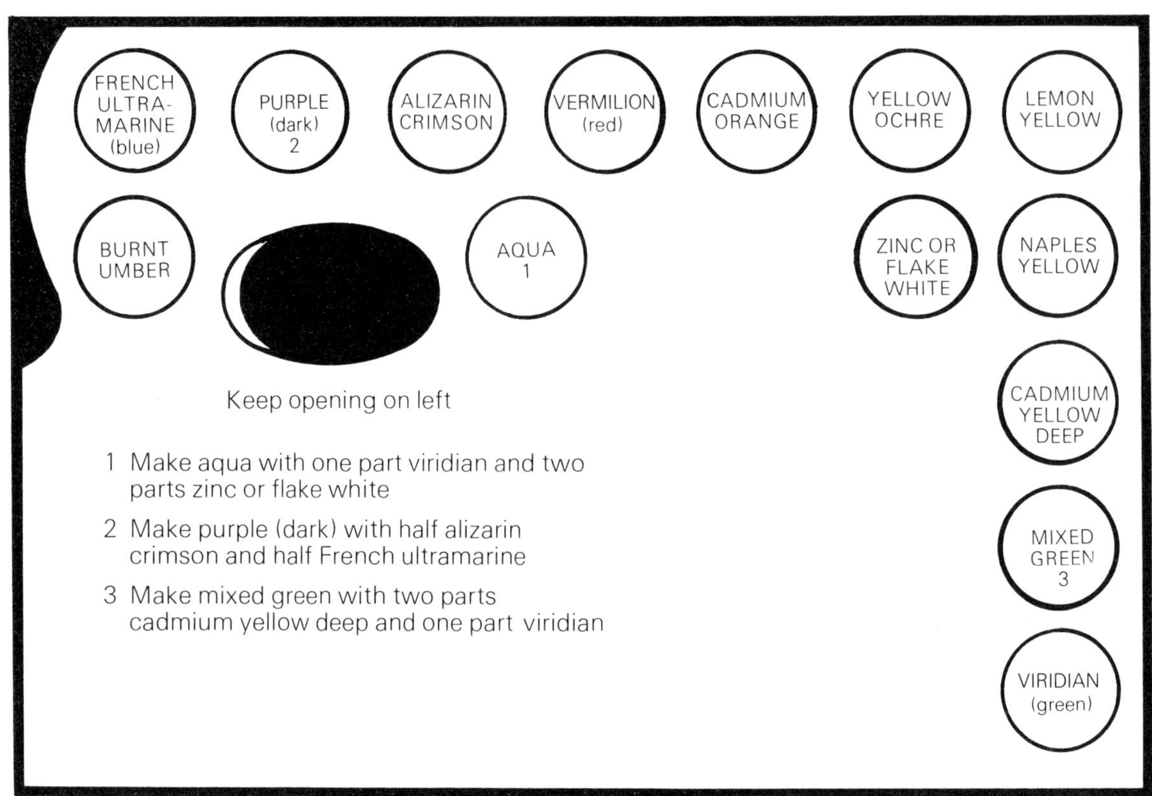

Set up your palette as shown above and opposite, using about a teaspoonful of each colour and mixing the aqua, purple and mixed green as instructed

colour on the canvas, put a small amount of paint on the tip of your knife or brush and cover the area required with short, sharp strokes to give a rough, raised texture. For dabbling, use a little more paint and, with the flat part of the top of the knife or brush, dab short strokes on the required area.

8 Six months after you have completed your painting, dust it off with a dry, soft paint brush and apply the clear varnish lightly. Lay the painting flat until dry — this will take about an hour.

9 One of the most difficult lessons to learn in painting is when to stop. You could argue that Albert P. Ryder, the famous American painter, reworked his paintings for thirty years in the solitude of his New York tenement. Painting over dust and grime gave a molten, jewel-like quality to his paintings. That's fine but, since it's quite possible that you may not be another Albert P. Ryder, forget it. In overworking, not only will your painting lose its spontaneity and freshness, but you may very well find that you lose the painting altogether.

All the materials illustrated opposite can be purchased in a complete Nancy Kominsky Paint Along Kit which has been made expressly to her specifications by George Rowney and Company Limited

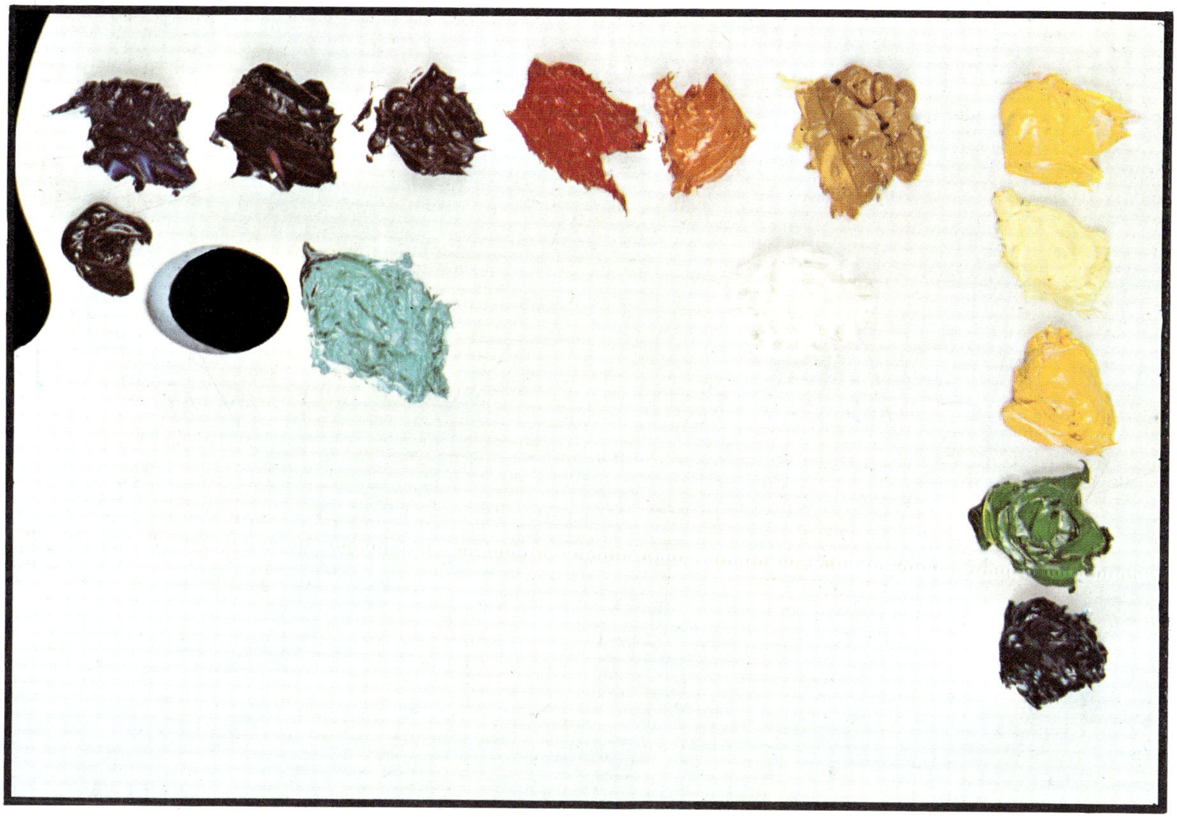

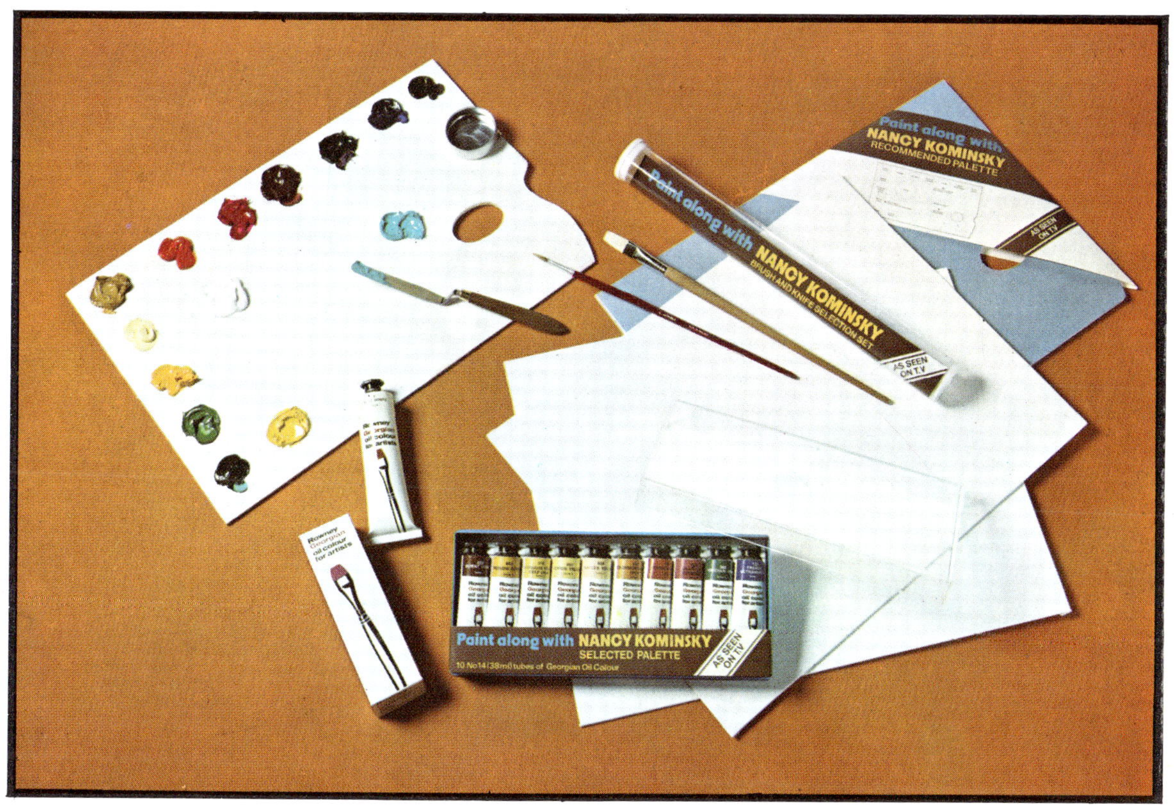

Paint along with
NANCY KOMINSKY
RECOMMENDED PALETTE
AS SEEN ON T.V.
Paint along with NANCY KOMINSKY
BRUSH AND KNIFE SELECTION SET
AS SEEN ON T.V.
Paint along with NANCY KOMINSKY
SELECTED PALETTE
AS SEEN ON T.V.
10 No.14 (38ml) tubes of Georgian Oil Colour

Gladioli

Florals are best for starters. Keep the painting simple.

THE DRAWING
1 Use canvas board, canvas or hardboard, 14 in. (36cm) by 18 in. (46cm) vertically.
2 Study the drawing and painting on pages 12 and 13.
3 Arrange the palette according to the palette layout on page 8.
4 Use the large, flat hog brush to stain the canvas with a light wash of burnt umber, as described in Step 1 on page 7. Wipe with toilet tissue.
5 With the medium round brush and dark umber wash put in the grid lines and simple drawing as indicated on page 12.
6 The light is coming from the left (note light on lower petals of flowers and buds), so with dark umber wash lightly shade in areas on upper half of flowers.
7 Clean your brushes in the medium of turpentine or white spirit.

THE PAINTING
Always mix paints with straight knife.

BACKGROUND (always painted in first)

Colour formula
Tones of greyed light green

light   medium   dark

Medium tone
1 tablespoon white
1 teaspoon yellow ochre
$\frac{1}{2}$ teaspoon mixed green
$\frac{1}{8}$ teaspoon vermilion
Mix and separate into three parts, one small ($\frac{1}{2}$ teaspoon) and two equal parts.
First part ($\frac{1}{2}$ teaspoon) for light tone
add $\frac{3}{4}$ teaspoon white
$\frac{1}{8}$ teaspoon yellow ochre

Second part for medium tone: do not touch

Third part for dark tone
add $\frac{1}{4}$ teaspoon purple
$\frac{1}{4}$ teaspoon mixed green

Clean your knife.

Let's paint
Use offset knife, held lightly.

1 Study the background in the painting on page 13.
2 Paint the background in thirds of light, medium and dark tones, starting on the right with dark tone.

3 Blend tones slightly and go around the flowers loosely. (The knife will feel awkward at first.) Clean knife.
4 With flat of knife lightly stroke on vermilion where indicated on background.
5 With the point of clean knife scratch in wet paint any stems and flowers lost.
6 Move left-over paint, if any, out of mixing area and clean the palette.
7 It is best to leave the background to dry before putting in the flowers.

PETALS

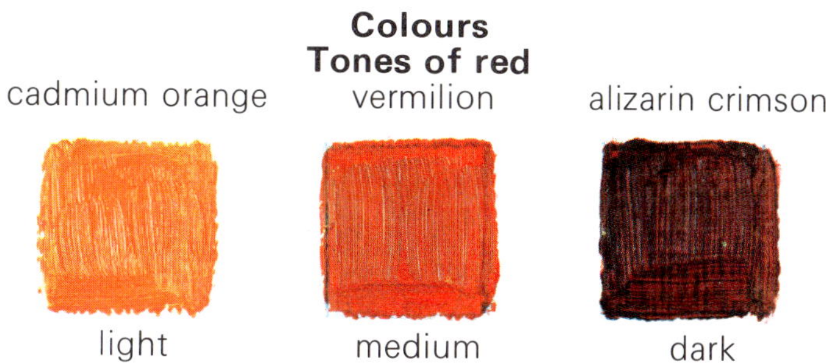

Colours
Tones of red

cadmium orange	vermilion	alizarin crimson
light	medium	dark

The above colours are used from the palette and require no mixing. However, you will need an additional tone which you mix in the following way:

Extra light tone
$\frac{1}{2}$ **teaspoon orange**
$\frac{1}{2}$ **teaspoon vermilion**
$\frac{1}{8}$ **teaspoon cadmium yellow deep**
$\frac{3}{4}$ **teaspoon white**

1 Study the painting on page 13. There are five stems with blooms. The rest are buds. Starting on the right of the canvas, stems one, three and five have dark blooms, and stems two and four have light blooms.
2 Using the flat of the knife, paint the top petals of blooms on stems one and three with alizarin crimson. Paint lower left petals of each bloom with vermilion and lower right petals with cadmium orange.
3 Paint blooms in profile on stem five with extra light tone on edge of petals and vermilion and alizarin crimson on the remaining area of the petals.
4 Paint top petals of blooms on stems two and four with vermilion. Paint the lower left petals with cadmium orange and lower right petals with extra light tone.
5 Stipple cadmium yellow deep from palette in centre of each bloom, for stamens.

continued on page 14

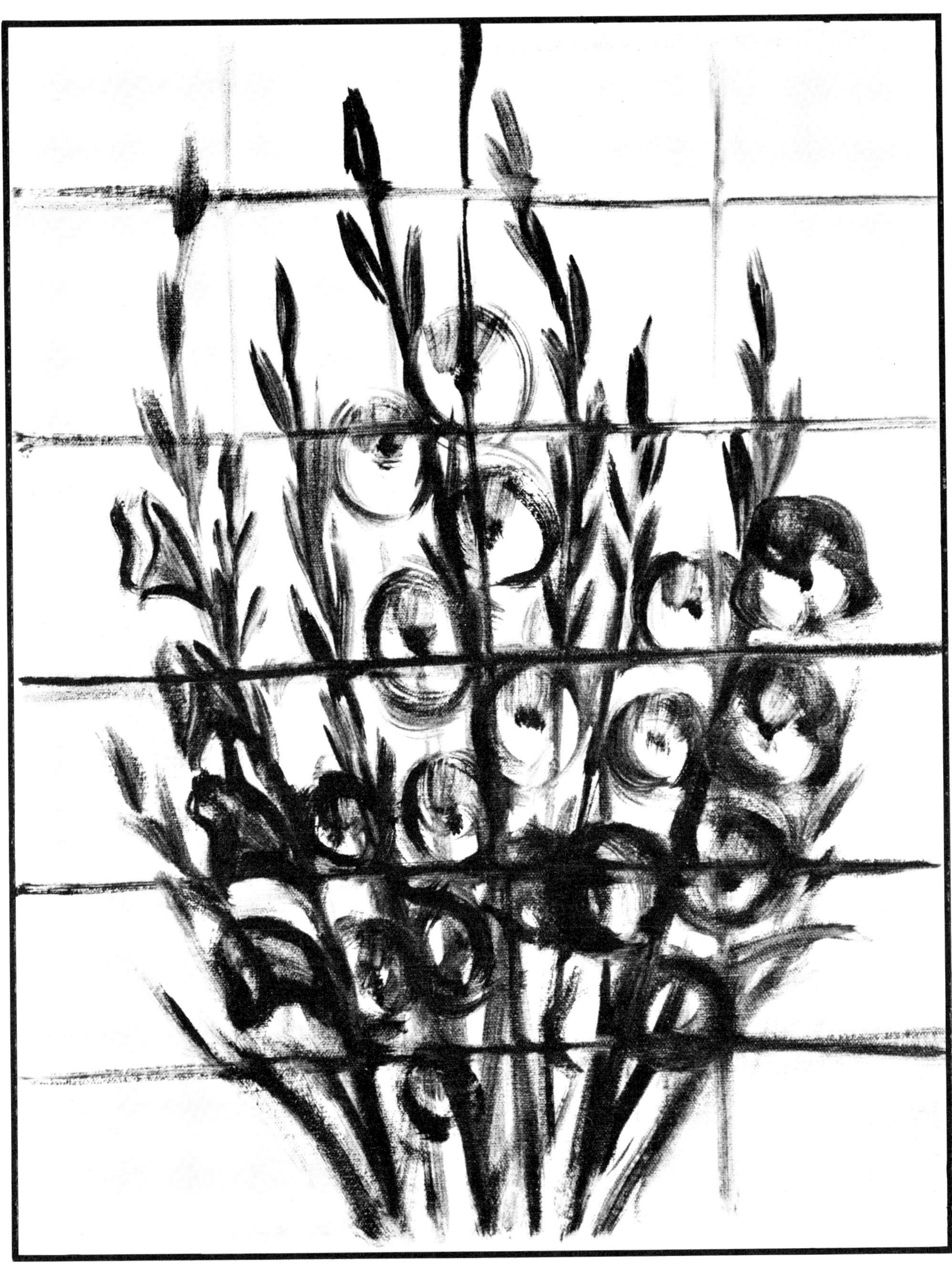

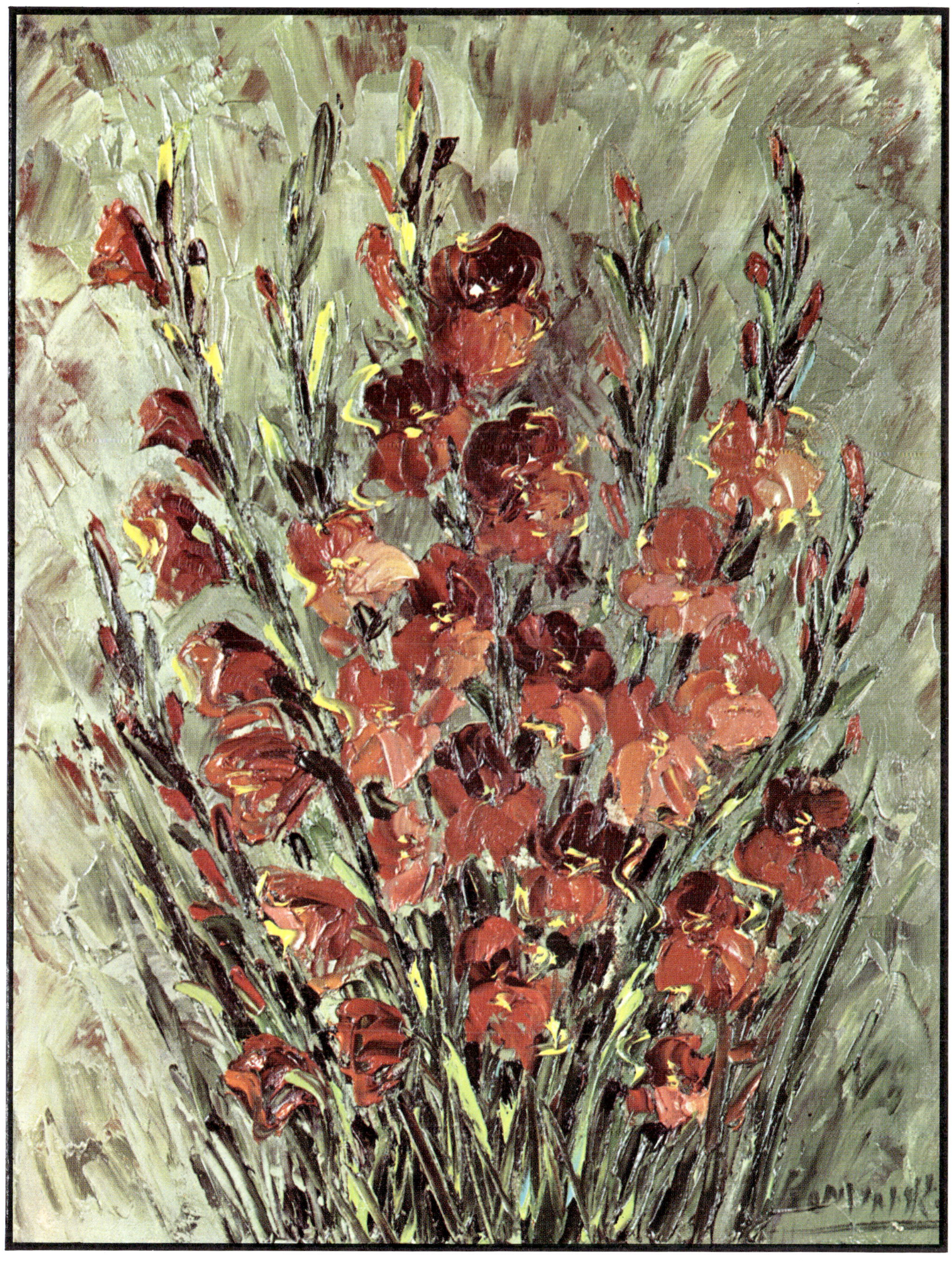

LEAVES, STEMS AND BUDS

Colour formula
Tones of green

 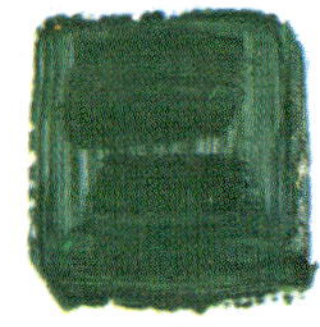 

light   medium   dark

Medium tone
1 tablespoon mixed green
½ teaspoon yellow ochre
¼ teaspoon vermilion
¼ teaspoon orange

Mix and separate into three parts, one small (½ teaspoon) and two equal parts.

First part (½ teaspoon) for light tone
add 1 teaspoon white
1 teaspoon lemon yellow

Second part for medium tone: do not touch

Third part for dark tone
add ¼ teaspoon purple
½ teaspoon mixed green

Clean your knife.

1 Study carefully the structure of the buds in the painting on the previous page.
2 Because this is your first painting, use the medium round brush instead of the knife for this stage. With dark tone lightly paint in all stems and buds.
3 The buds on the right of the stems are mostly dark, so add just a little medium tone. Tip the buds with vermilion.
4 Paint a little light tone on the buds on the left of the stems. Tip them with vermilion and a touch of cadmium orange.
5 Paint a little light tone on the stems at base of flowers, then add a few strokes of purple and aqua where indicated.
6 Put in a few spiky leaves where indicated — dark tone on the right of stems and light tone on the left.
7 Finish with a few touches of lemon yellow on stems and around edges of blooms.

Clean palette, brushes and knives.

You can now look forward to doing the other paintings in the book, as you view the marvellous result of this, your first painting of the series.

Wine and Fruit

THE DRAWING

1 Use canvas board, canvas or hardboard, 14 in. (36cm) by 18 in. (46cm) vertically.
2 Study the drawing and painting on pages 16 and 17.
3 Arrange the palette according to the palette layout on page 8.
4 Use the large, flat hog brush to stain the canvas with a light wash of burnt umber, as described in Step 1 on page 7. Wipe with toilet tissue.
5 With the medium round brush and dark umber wash put in the grid lines and simple drawing as indicated on page 16. (Do not draw grapes too large or round.)
6 The light is coming from the left (note highlights on the left side of the bottle, glass, vase and fruit), so with dark umber wash lightly shade the right side of these objects.
7 Clean your brushes in the medium of turpentine or white spirit.

THE PAINTING
Always mix paints with straight knife.

BACKGROUND

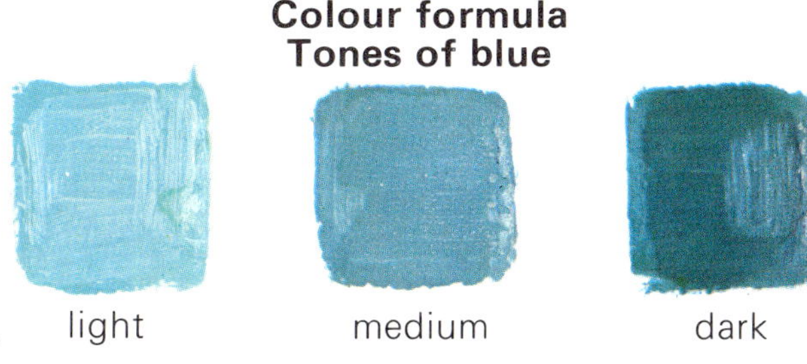

Medium tone
1 teaspoon white
$\frac{3}{4}$ teaspoon aqua
$\frac{1}{2}$ teaspoon blue
$\frac{1}{4}$ teaspoon orange
$\frac{1}{8}$ teaspoon mixed green

Mix and separate into three parts, one small ($\frac{1}{2}$ teaspoon) and two equal parts.

First part ($\frac{1}{2}$ teaspoon) for light tone
add $\frac{3}{4}$ teaspoon white
$\frac{1}{4}$ teaspoon Naples yellow
$\frac{1}{2}$ teaspoon aqua

Second part for medium tone: do not touch

Third part for dark tone
add $\frac{1}{2}$ teaspoon blue
$\frac{3}{4}$ teaspoon aqua
$\frac{1}{2}$ teaspoon orange

Clean your knife.

Let's paint
Use offset knife, held lightly.

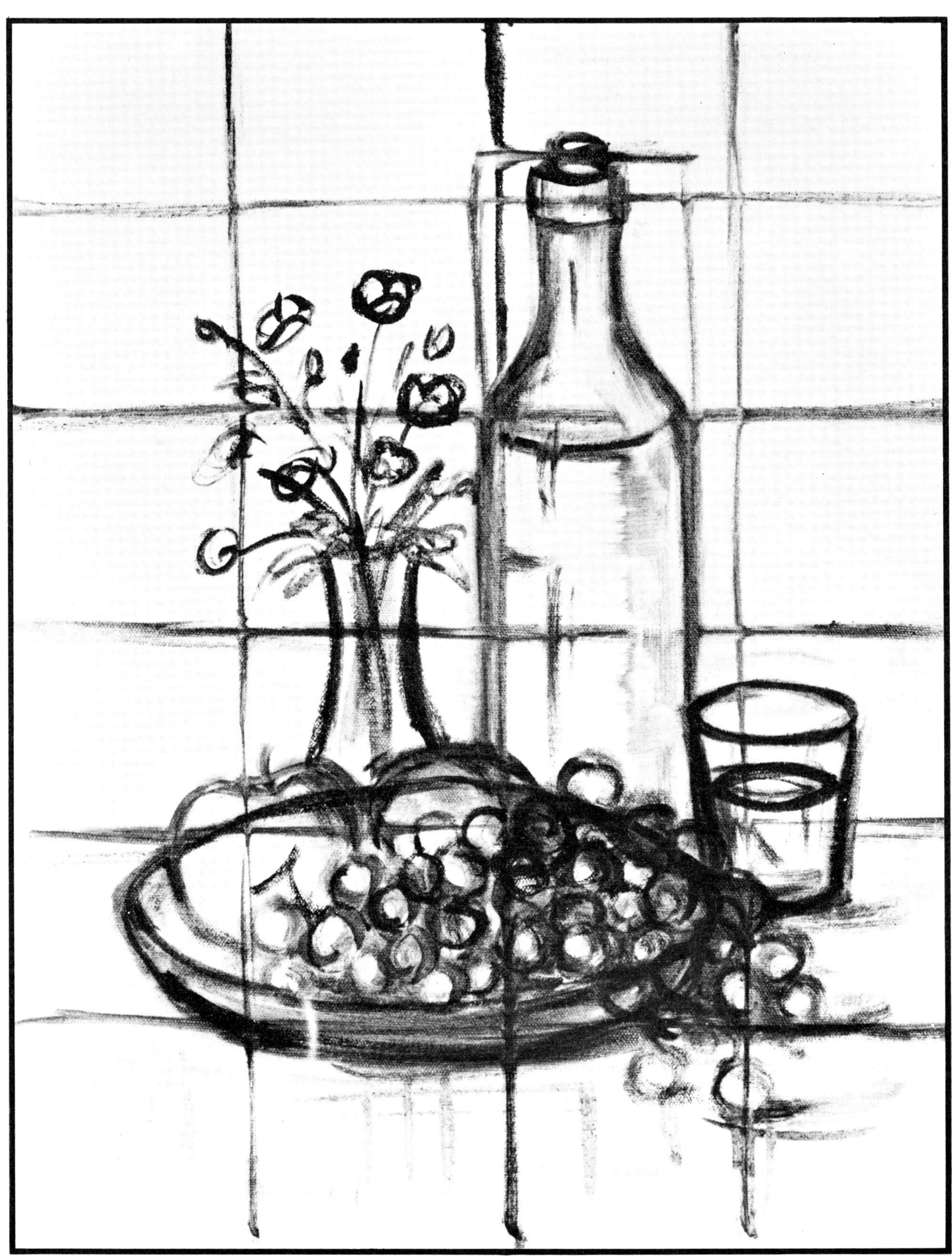

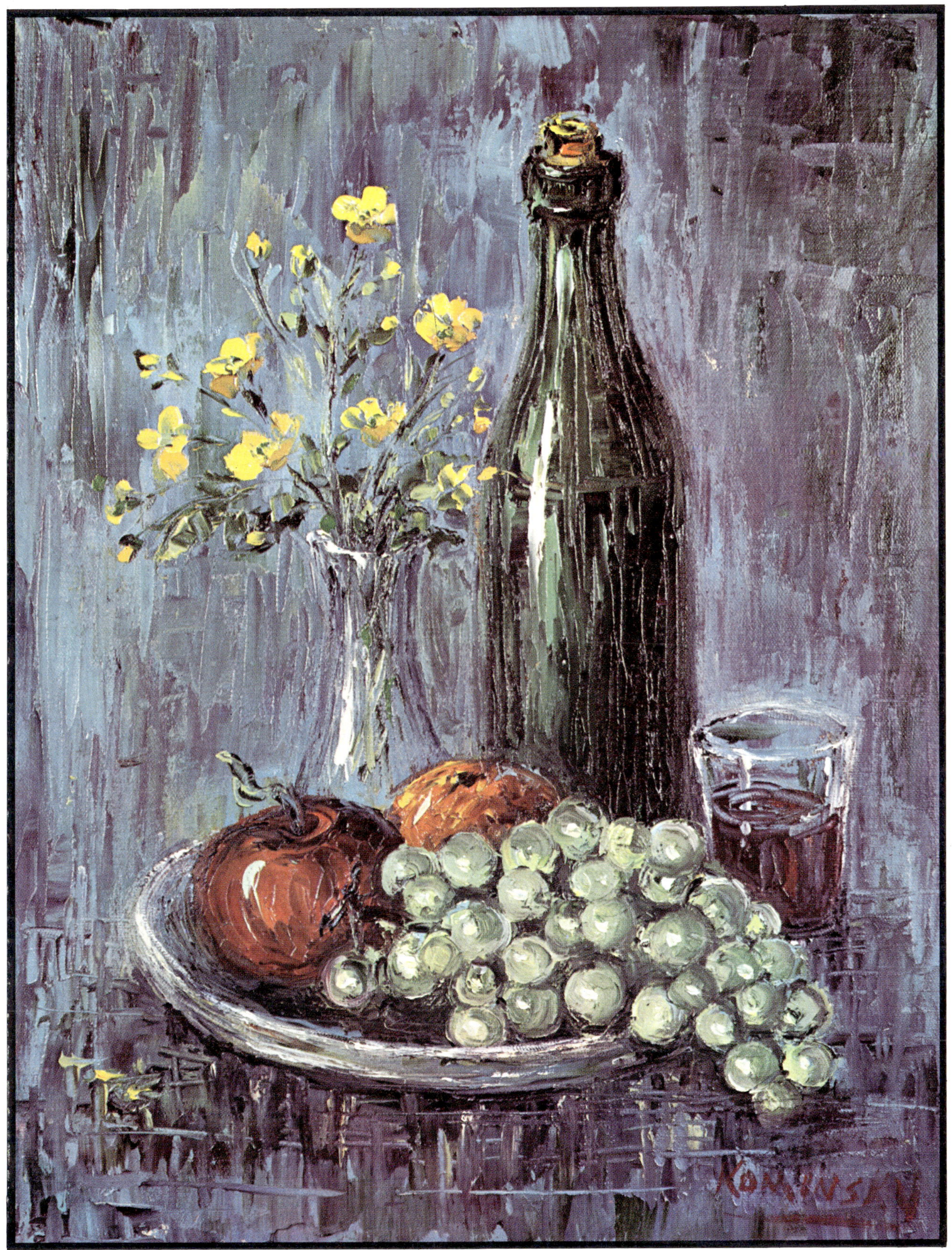

1 Study the painting on the previous page.
2 Paint in background, starting with the dark tone on the right. Use long strokes, with the flat of the knife. Paint medium tone in the centre and light tone on the left. Paint out flowers for now, as they can be added later (but scratch the shapes in wet paint if you like). Go around objects carefully.
3 With purple from palette, paint under objects to form shadows. Using the flat of the knife lightly drag the purple in downward strokes. Then, with the tip of clean knife scratch over this with horizontal strokes to make reflections.
4 Lightly stroke a little alizarin crimson and viridian green from the palette on the background where indicated.

VASE, FRUIT BOWL AND WINE GLASS
1 Because these objects are glass, the background is seen through them. Carefully paint medium blue tone through vase, preserving outline.
2 Paint fruit bowl with the same medium tone, again preserving outline. Use round strokes in the shape of the bowl.
3 With dark blue tone paint through wine glass in the same way.
4 Outline the above objects lightly with purple, emphasising individual forms. All highlights will be added later.

WINE BOTTLE

**Colour formula
Tones of green**

 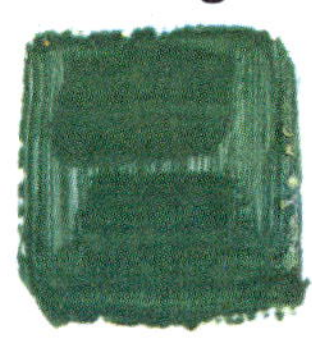 

light   medium   dark

Refer to page 14 for tones of green and mix according to the directions.

1 Study the painting on the previous page.
2 Paint right side of wine bottle with dark tone, taking care with the lip.
3 Paint medium tone in the middle of the bottle.
4 Paint light tone on the left of the bottle, and edge it with medium tone.
5 Paint a few strokes of viridian green from palette on right side and at the bottom of the bottle, behind fruit. Blend lightly.
6 Outline right side of bottle with purple, then add a few light strokes of alizarin crimson.
7 Paint a few strokes of purple on left side of bottle.
8 Outline lip of bottle carefully with purple.
9 With clean knife, scratch in a curved horizontal line across the bottle where it starts to broaden out.
10 Paint the cork with yellow ochre from palette. Outline it with purple, then add a highlight on top of cadmium yellow deep. Finish with a tiny stroke of cadmium orange across the middle of the cork.

The remaining tones of green will be used for the grapes, and for the leaves and stems of the flowers.

ORANGE

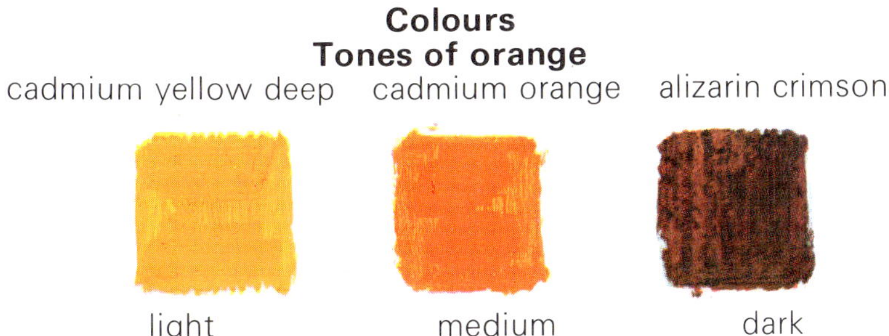

Colours
Tones of orange

cadmium yellow deep   cadmium orange   alizarin crimson

light   medium   dark

The above colours are used from the palette and require no mixing.

1 Paint dark tone on right side of orange, using stippling strokes.
2 Paint medium tone on rest of orange, using the same strokes.
3 Paint a highlight of cadmium yellow deep on the left side, and add a spot of dark
   green tone for the stalk.

APPLE

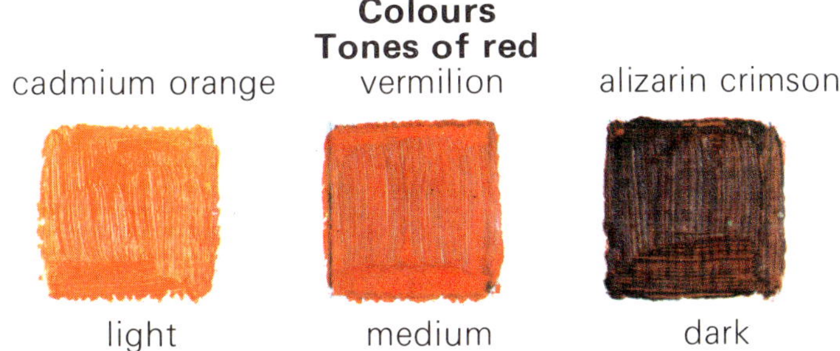

Colours
Tones of red

cadmium orange   vermilion   alizarin crimson

light   medium   dark

The above colours are used from the palette and require no mixing.

1 Paint the right side and bottom of apple with dark tone, using round strokes.
2 Paint the centre of apple with medium tone, using the same stroke. Preserve stalk area
   by painting around right side of it with this same medium tone.
3 Paint left side of apple with light tone. Blend tones lightly.
4 Paint stalk with purple, then add a few strokes of dark and light green tones on the
   left side of it.

WINE IN GLASS

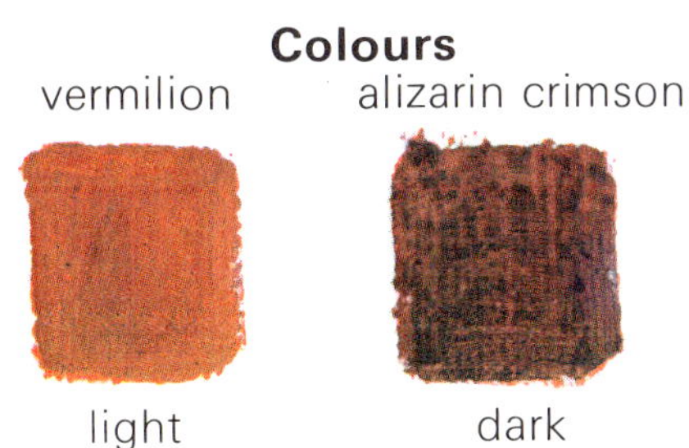

Colours

vermilion   alizarin crimson

light   dark

The above colours are used from the palette and require no mixing.

1 Paint dark tone in the glass where indicated.
2 With edge of clean knife, scratch two half-circles into dark tone, following the shape of the rim of the glass. Don't overwork it — give just a suggestion.
3 Paint a rather long stroke of light tone on top of the dark tone near centre, for highlight.

GRAPES
These can look like marbles, so be careful.

To some of the remaining tones of green used for the wine bottle, make the following additions to give the colours required for the grapes. Keep left-over tones of green for stems and leaves of flowers.

Light tone

to $\frac{1}{2}$ teaspoon light green tone
add $\frac{3}{4}$ teaspoon white
$\frac{1}{2}$ teaspoon Naples yellow

Medium tone

to $\frac{1}{2}$ teaspoon medium green tone
add $\frac{1}{2}$ teaspoon white
$\frac{1}{4}$ teaspoon yellow ochre

Dark tone

to $\frac{1}{2}$ teaspoon dark green tone
add $\frac{1}{2}$ teaspoon white
$\frac{1}{8}$ teaspoon yellow ochre

1 Study grapes carefully in the painting on page 17.
2 Using round strokes paint the grapes on the right side and top of bunch with dark tone on the right side of each grape and medium tone on the left side.
3 Paint the grapes in the front with medium tone on the right and light tone on the left.
4 Paint a few darker grapes here and there as indicated with dark tone.
5 Loosely outline the grapes with purple on right side and between them.
6 Touch right side of grapes with a bit of light blue tone. Highlights will be added later.
7 Paint purple under the fruit in the bowl, for shadow.

BUTTERCUPS

Colours
Tones of yellow

lemon yellow   cadmium yellow deep   yellow ochre

light   medium   dark

The above colours are used from the palette and require no mixing.

1 Study carefully the structure of the flowers in the painting on page 17. Keep them delicate and dainty.
2 Paint flowers in blobs of the three yellow tones. Paint upper left petal with medium tone.
3 Paint upper right petal with light tone.

4 Paint front petals with dark tone.
5 Paint touches of medium and light tones in bottom lefthand corner of canvas, for an impression of fallen petals.

STEMS AND LEAVES
For these you will need the left-over tones of green used for the wine bottle.

1 With medium round brush and dark tone, paint in delicate stems. Add a little light tone here and there. Do not paint too many in the vase.
2 Paint in a few delicate leaves with dark tone and edge them with light tone.
3 Paint tiny, dainty buds with light tone, then tip them with cadmium yellow deep.
4 Put a spot of light tone in centre of each flower, for stamens.
5 Lightly stroke a little light tone on the left of the background and under fruit bowl, for reflections.

HIGHLIGHTS

Colour tone
$\frac{1}{2}$ teaspoon white
$\frac{1}{4}$ teaspoon Naples yellow

1 Paint highlights, as indicated, on left side and top of vase, on wine bottle and on rim, edges and just off centre of glass.
2 Carefully outline fruit bowl with above colour tone.
3 Add highlights to apple, orange and grapes, where indicated.

Clean palette, brushes and knives.

Your beautiful still life is finished. Actually, a little swig of the wine at the beginning will give a more relaxed painting!

Bonnie Banks

THE DRAWING
1 Use canvas board, canvas or hardboard, 14 in. (36cm) by 18 in. (46cm) horizontally.
2 Study the drawing and painting on pages 24 and 25.
3 Arrange the palette according to the palette layout on page 8.
4 Use the large, flat hog brush to stain the canvas with a light wash of burnt umber, as described in Step 1 on page 7. Wipe with toilet tissue.
5 With the medium round brush and dark umber wash put in the grid lines and simple drawing as indicated on page 24. Draw in only tree trunks for now, as the foliage will be added later.
6 The light is coming from the left, so with dark umber wash lightly shade in areas on the right of mountains, trees and ground.
7 Clean your brushes in the medium of turpentine or white spirit.

THE PAINTING

SKY

**Colour formula
Sky tones**

 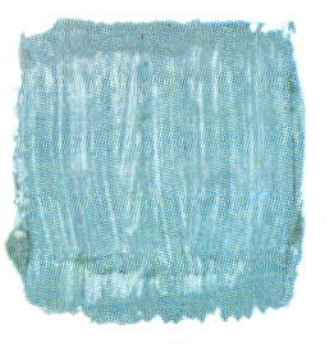 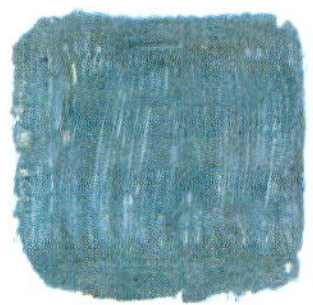

light   medium   dark

**Medium tone
1 tablespoon white
$\frac{1}{2}$ teaspoon aqua
$\frac{1}{4}$ teaspoon blue
$\frac{1}{4}$ teaspoon orange**

Mix and separate into three parts, one small ($\frac{1}{2}$ teaspoon) and two equal parts.

**First part ($\frac{1}{2}$ teaspoon) for light tone
add   1 teaspoon white
$\frac{3}{4}$ teaspoon Naples yellow**

Second part for medium tone: do not touch

**Third part for dark tone
add $\frac{1}{8}$ teaspoon blue
$\frac{1}{4}$ teaspoon aqua
$\frac{1}{4}$ teaspoon orange
$\frac{1}{8}$ teaspoon purple**

Clean your knife.

In this painting only the light and medium tones are used for the sky. The dark tone is used for the mountains.

Let's paint
Use offset knife, held lightly.

1 Study the sky in the painting on page 25.
2 Paint light tone around the top of the mountains and up into part of the sky. Use the flat of the knife, as the point makes ridges.
3 Paint remaining sky with medium tone, dragging the colour from top of canvas down to mountains in a slanting stroke. Blend the tones but take care not to lose tonal values. Retain light tone around the mountains.

MOUNTAINS

**Colour tones
to each of the light, medium and dark sky tones
add $\frac{1}{8}$ teaspoon purple**

1 Paint the right side of the mountains on the righthand side of the canvas with dark tone just mixed. Use long, flowing strokes.

2 Paint dark tone in the water along the base of the mountains, for reflections.
3 Paint left side of righthand mountains with medium tone.
4 Paint the smaller mountains on the lefthand side of canvas with medium tone on the right and light tone on the left.
5 Clean knife, then drag a bit of sky into the mountains to soften the line.

WATER

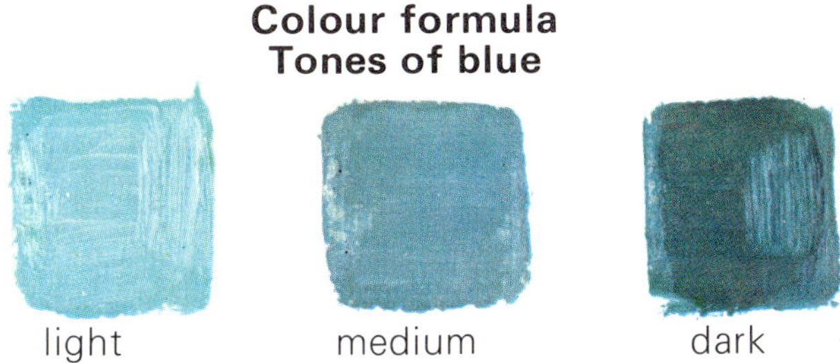

**Colour formula
Tones of blue**

light   medium   dark

Refer to page 15 for tones of blue and mix according to the directions.

1 Study the painting on page 25.
2 Paint strokes of dark tone on the right side of canvas. The strokes should go straight across and be slightly dipped. Make sure the water does not go uphill or downhill.
3 Start blending in medium tone, going behind dark hills on the left. Overlap the mountains a little and blend lightly.
4 Paint light tone on left and centre of water, blending slightly.
5 Add $\frac{1}{2}$ teaspoon white and $\frac{1}{4}$ teaspoon Naples yellow to light tone. Paint this tone down centre of water to give an extra sparkle of light.

YELLOW GRASSES

**Colour formula
Tones of yellow ochre**

light   medium   dark

**Medium tone
1 tablespoon yellow ochre
$\frac{1}{2}$ teaspoon white
$\frac{1}{2}$ teaspoon lemon yellow**

Mix and separate into three parts, one small ($\frac{1}{2}$ teaspoon) and two equal parts.

**First part ($\frac{1}{2}$ teaspoon) for light tone
add   1 teaspoon white
$\frac{1}{2}$ teaspoon lemon yellow**

Second part for medium tone: do not touch

**Third part for dark tone
add $\frac{1}{2}$ teaspoon purple**

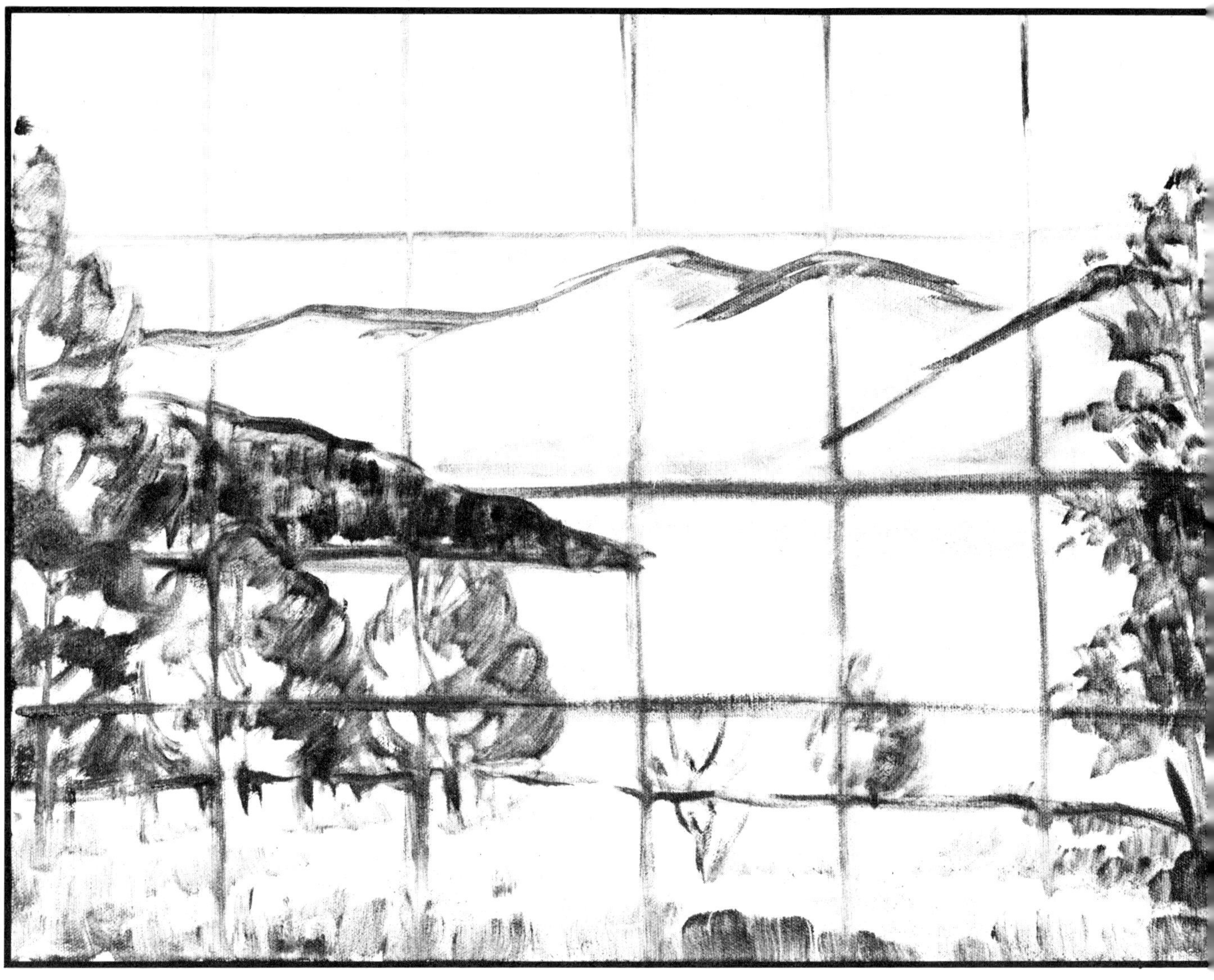

1 Study the painting opposite.
2 Paint dark tone along the bottom of canvas. Keep your strokes uneven and textured. Paint some strokes of purple here and there, where indicated. Then add a few strokes of medium blue tone and cadmium orange.
3 Paint with medium yellow ochre tone next, working towards the shoreline. Blend slightly and go through the trees.
4 Paint the grasses along the shoreline with light yellow ochre tone. (It is uneven with a high point in the centre.) Go out over the water a trifle.
5 With clean knife, scratch the edges of the grasses to break up the mass.

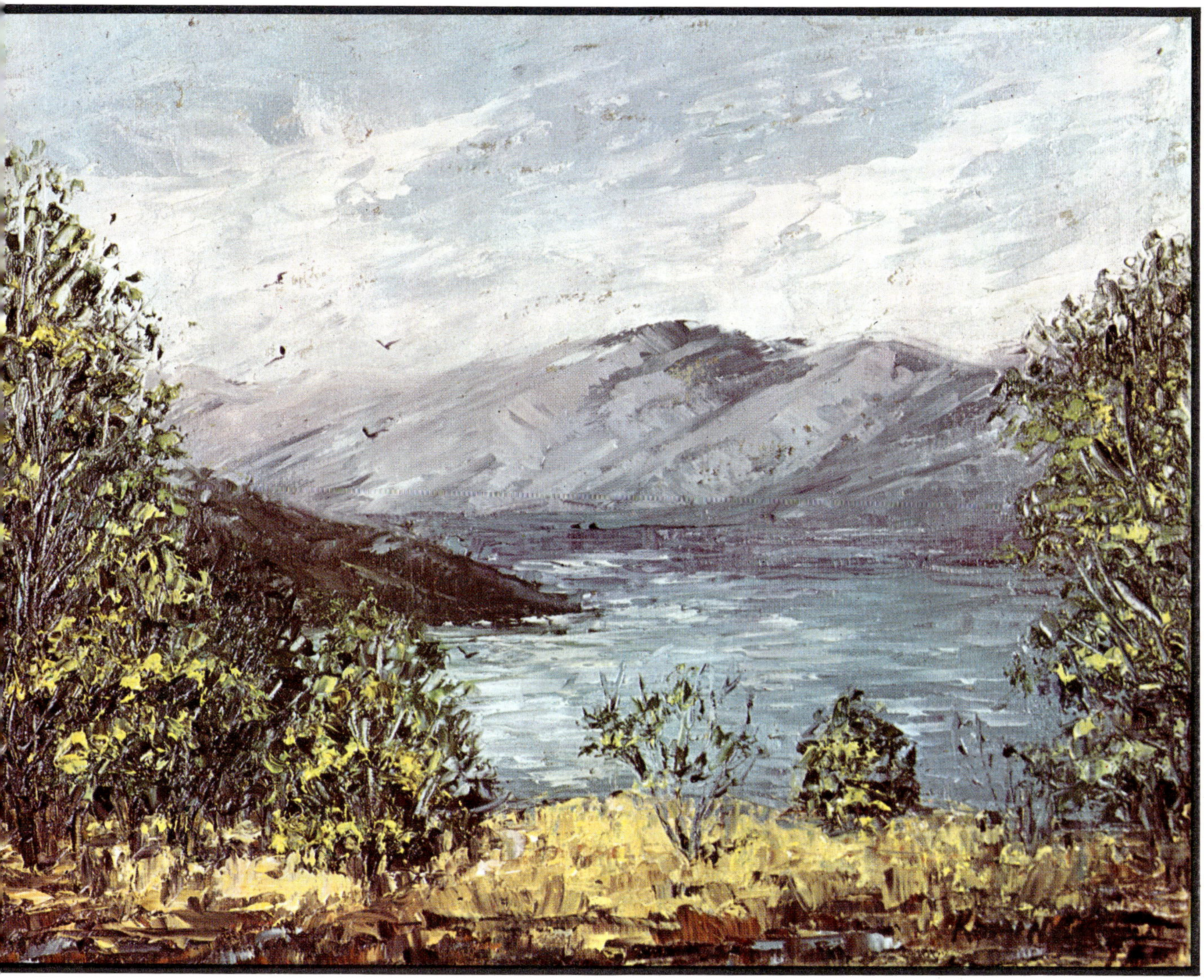

DARK HILL, TREES AND SHRUBS

**Colour formula
Tones of green**

  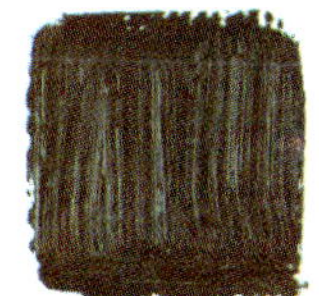

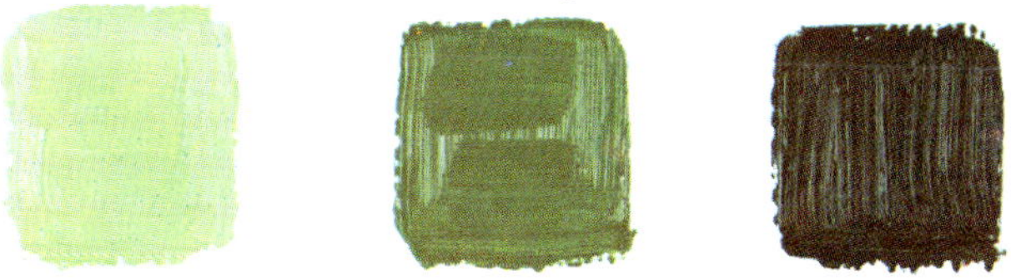

light   medium   dark

Refer to page 14 for tones of green and mix according to the directions. You will also need an additional tone which you mix in the following way:

Extra dark tone
to   ½ teaspoon dark green tone
add ½ teaspoon dark mountain colour tone

1. Study the painting on the previous page.
2. Paint the dark hill in the lake with extra dark tone.
3. Paint a few strokes of dark tone used for the mountains across the top of hill. With clean knife blend base of hill with water.
4. Paint tree trunks and branches thickly with purple. Add a few touches of aqua on the trunk on the left of canvas.
5. You may prefer to use the medium round brush for branches — paint them in lightly, again with purple. Do not paint too many and take care to keep them delicate.
6. Paint the foliage and shrubs with dark green tone on the right. Use dabbling strokes and go across branches in masses.
7. Paint medium green tone partly over the dark tone, using the same strokes. Keep branches showing in places.
8. Paint light green tone mostly on left of trees but still going across trees where indicated.
9. Paint purple at base of foliage of trees.
10. With a little purple scratch in a couple of bare shrubs where indicated.
11. Paint a little lemon yellow from palette on left side of all trees, to give an extra highlight.
12. With tip of knife and purple carefully paint in a few flying birds.

Clean palette, brushes and knives.

Landscapes are charming, and I'm sure it's getting easier. Keep painting.

Grey Day at Blackwall

THE DRAWING

1 Use canvas board, canvas or hardboard, 14 in. (36cm) by 18 in. (46cm) vertically.
2 Study the drawing and painting on pages 28 and 29.
3 Arrange the palette according to the palette layout on page 8.
4 Use the large, flat hog brush to stain the canvas with a light wash of burnt umber, as described in Step 1 on page 7. Wipe with toilet tissue.
5 With the medium round brush and dark umber wash put in the grid lines and simple drawing as indicated on page 28. (Don't put in rigging on the large boat.)
6 The light is coming from the sky and the right, so with dark umber wash lightly shade in areas where indicated.
7 Clean your brushes in the medium of turpentine or white spirit.

THE PAINTING

SKY

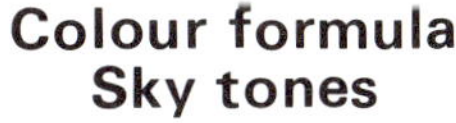

**Colour formula
Sky tones**

<table>
<tr><td>light</td><td>medium</td><td>dark</td></tr>
</table>

Refer to page 22 for sky tones and mix according to the directions. You will also need an additional tone which you mix in the following way:

Extra light tone
to $\frac{1}{4}$ **teaspoon light sky tone**
add   **1 teaspoon white**
      $\frac{1}{2}$ **teaspoon Naples yellow**

Clean your knife.

Let's paint
Use offset knife, held lightly.

1 Study the painting on page 29.
2 Paint extra light tone around buildings and up into the sky.
3 Blend in the light tone, watching strokes. Leave light area where indicated.
4 Paint medium tone across the top and down into the light tone, taking care not to slant strokes sharply.
5 Paint a few slanting strokes of dark tone at the top of the canvas.
6 The green tone in the sky will be added later.

BUILDINGS

1 Study the painting on page 29.
2 Paint left side of buildings with medium sky tone and right side with light tone.
3 Paint a few dark buildings with dark sky tone. Keep them indefinite.

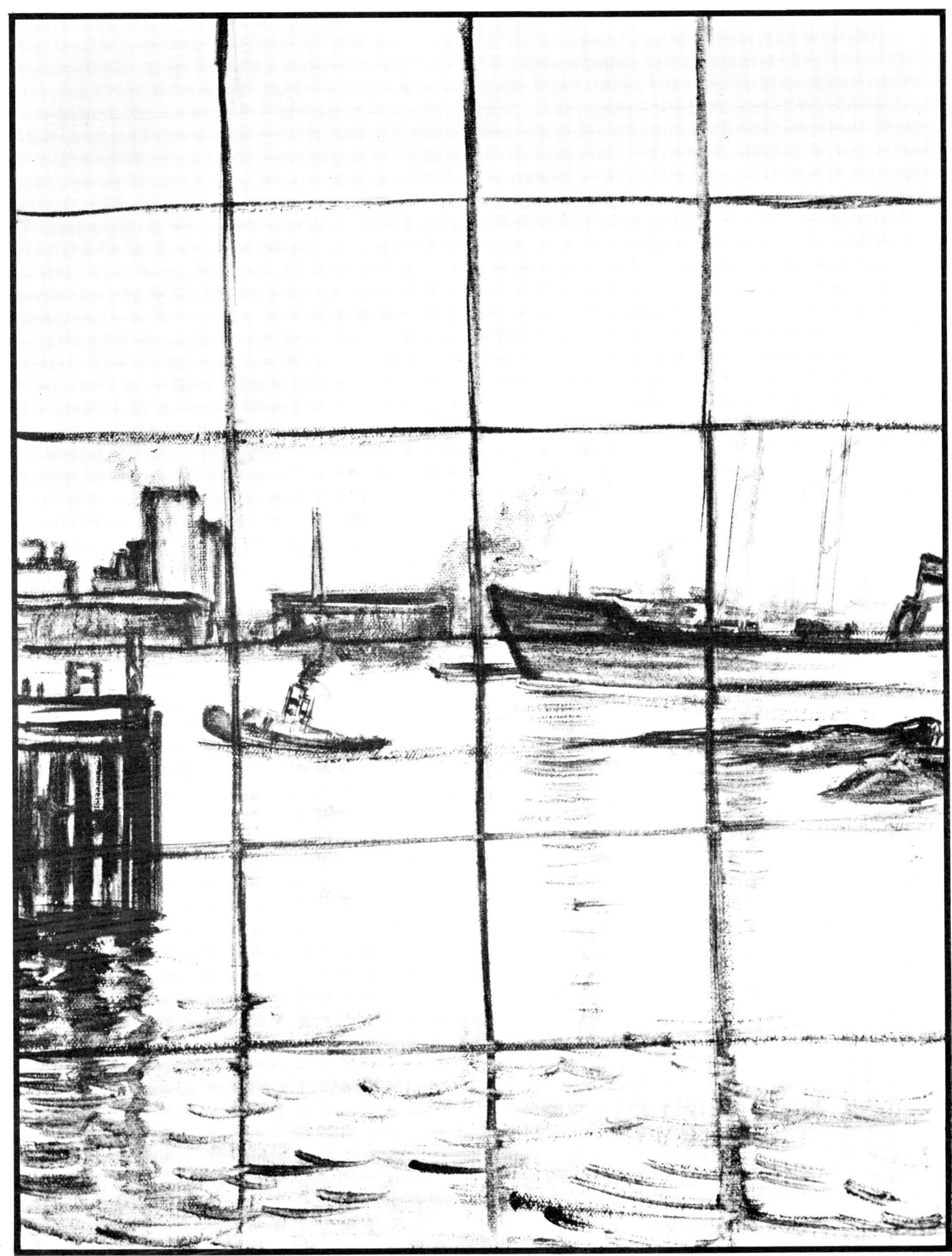

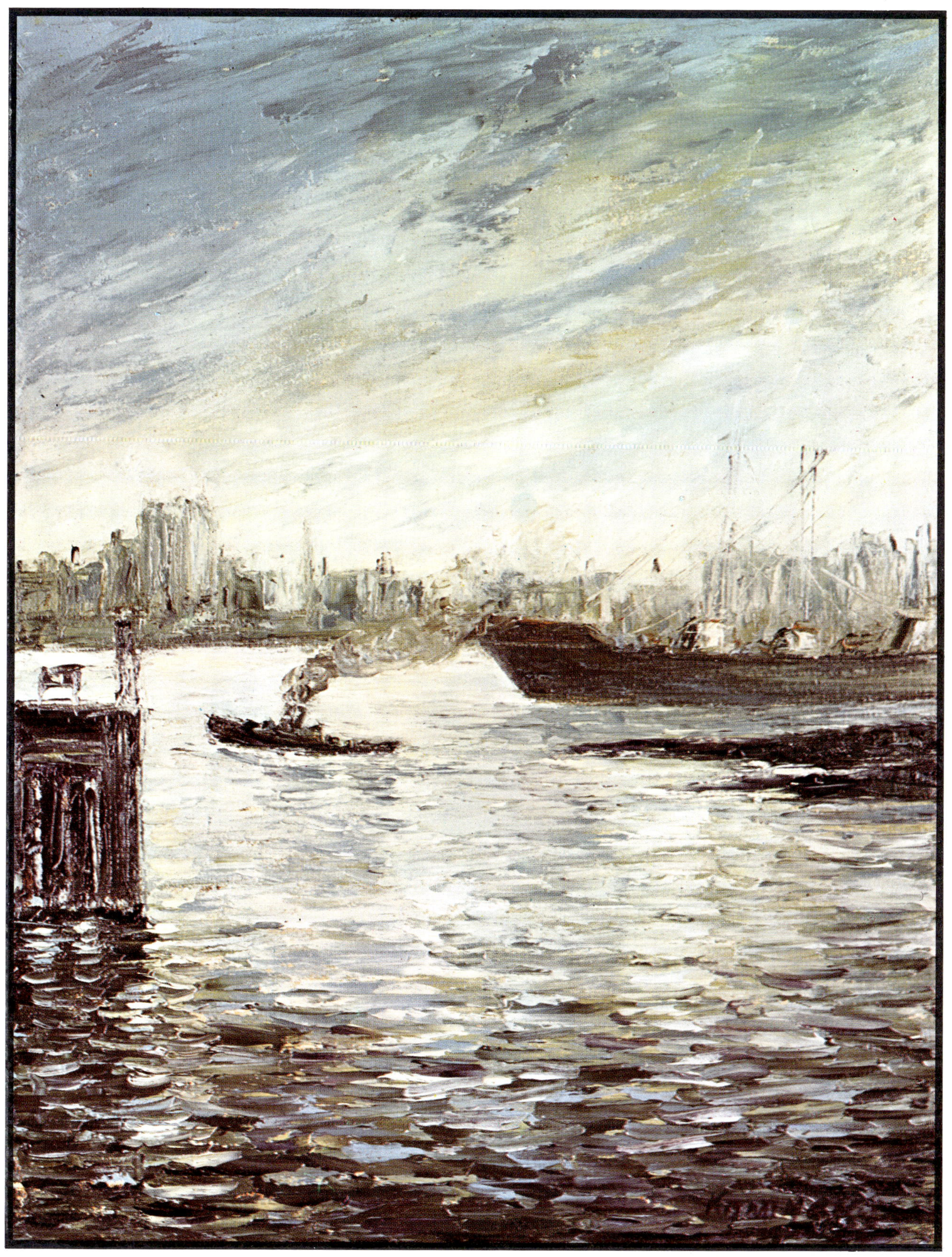

WATER
The tones already mixed for the sky, together with tones of greyed dark green will be used for the water. You may have to mix another half-batch of sky tones including the extra light tone.

Colour formula
Tones of greyed dark green

light   medium   dark

Medium tone
1 tablespoon yellow ochre
$\frac{1}{2}$ teaspoon mixed green
$\frac{1}{2}$ teaspoon purple
Mix and separate into three parts, one small ($\frac{1}{2}$ teaspoon) and two equal parts.
First part ($\frac{1}{2}$ teaspoon) for light tone
add   1 teaspoon white
$\frac{1}{8}$ teaspoon yellow ochre

Second part for medium tone: do not touch

Third part for dark tone
add $\frac{1}{2}$ teaspoon purple
$\frac{1}{4}$ teaspoon viridian
$\frac{1}{4}$ teaspoon yellow ochre

1 Study the painting on the previous page.
2 Paint extra light sky tone along near the base of the buildings, using short strokes going straight across and slightly dipping. Make sure that the water does not go uphill or downhill.
3 Paint all the light areas first, where indicated, using the same extra light tone.
4 Paint light and medium sky tones alternately in the areas in between.
5 The water under the pier on the left of the canvas is very dark, so paint short strokes of purple and alternate with dark greyed dark green tones. Take these strokes to the bottom of the canvas. Paint in a few strokes of medium sky tone where indicated.
6 Paint water at the bottom of the canvas alternately with dark and medium greyed dark green tones, dark sky tone and purple. Retain tonal values.
7 Paint a few strokes of light greyed dark green tone up into the medium and light tones.
8 With flat of knife, carefully paint a little medium and light greyed dark green tones into the sky and buildings where indicated.
9 Paint the two dark areas of water on the right of the canvas with purple and dark greyed dark green tone.

LARGE BOAT

Colour tone
to $\frac{1}{4}$ teaspoon medium greyed dark green tone
add $\frac{1}{4}$ teaspoon dark sky tone

1 Study the painting on page 29.
2 Paint the large boat with the tone just mixed, using long, horizontal strokes.
3 Add a few strokes of light greyed dark green tone on the right of the boat.
4 Paint the superstructure with the tone just mixed on the left and extra light sky tone on the right.
5 Add a few touches of cadmium orange on the boat where indicated.
6 With the point of clean knife delicately scratch in the masts and rigging.
7 With the flat of clean knife blend bottom of boat with water.

FERRY BOAT
1 Study the painting on page 29.
2 Paint the ferry boat with a mixture of purple and dark greyed dark green tone. Retain form, and do not make the boat too large.
3 Paint a trickle of extra light sky tone under boat for wake.
4 Add a little white to the tone mixed for the ferry boat, and use this to paint in the smoke. Use the medium round brush for this. (It would, in fact, be easier to add the smoke when the painting is dry.)

PIER
1 Study the painting on page 29.
2 Paint pier with purple, keeping piles separate, so that the water shows through.

This will be a favourite painting, especially with men. Keep painting.

Wind on Exmoor

THE DRAWING
1 Use canvas board, canvas or hardboard, 14 in. (36cm) by 18 in. (46cm) vertically.
2 Study the drawing and painting on pages 32 and 33.
3 Arrange the palette according to the palette layout on page 8.
4 Use the large, flat hog brush to stain the canvas with a light wash of burnt umber, as described in Step 1 on page 7. Wipe with toilet tissue.
5 With the medium round brush and dark umber wash put in the grid lines and simple drawing as indicated on page 32. Study the perspective of the house and fence, and the angle of the road.
6 The light is coming from the left, so with dark umber wash lightly shade the right of the house, and the foreground of the road and ground.
7 Clean your brushes in the medium of turpentine or white spirit.

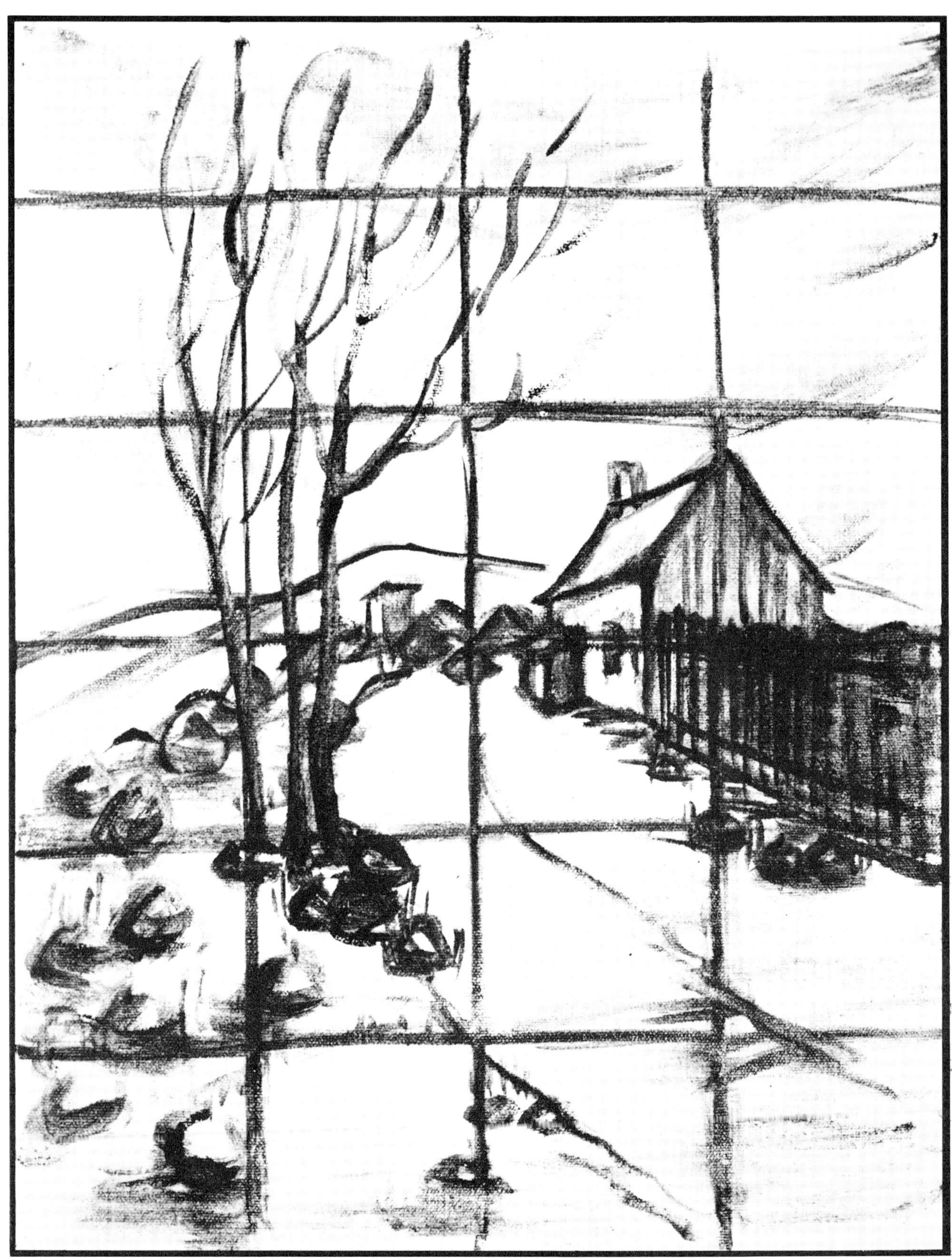

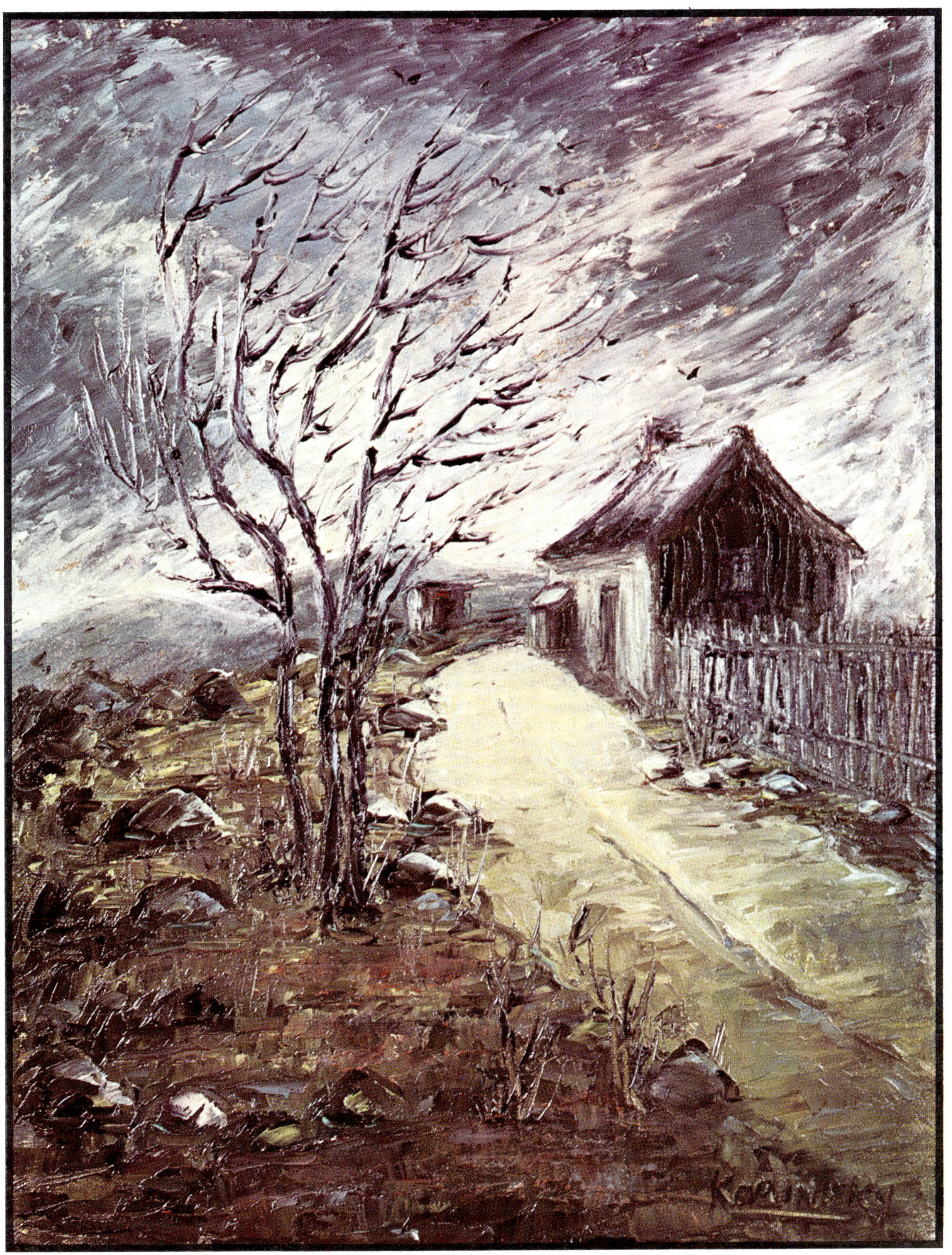

Kazinsky

THE PAINTING

SKY AND HILLS

**Colour formula
Sky tones**

  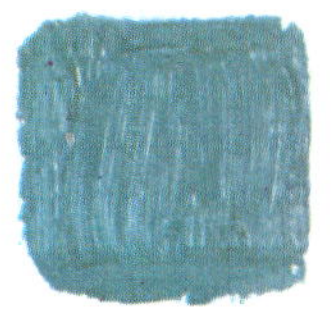

light   medium   dark

Refer to page 22 for sky tones and mix according to the directions. You will also need two additional tones which you mix in the following way:

Extra light tone
to $\frac{1}{4}$ **teaspoon light sky tone**
add $\frac{1}{2}$ **teaspoon white**
$\frac{1}{4}$ **teaspoon Naples yellow**
touch of orange

Extra dark tone
to $\frac{1}{2}$ **teaspoon dark sky tone**
add $\frac{1}{8}$ **teaspoon purple**
touch of orange

Clean your knife.

Let's paint
Use offset knife, held lightly.

1　Study the painting on the previous page. Paint out branches of trees for now.
2　Paint extra light tone around hills and in the sky where indicated.
3　Paint light tone going up into sky and out towards each corner of the canvas.
4　Paint dark and extra dark tones at the top, left and right of the canvas. Keep tones separated to create dramatic contrasts.
5　Paint the hills with dark tone.
6　Paint a little light tone on the right side of the hills. Blend tones lightly.

HOUSE

**Colour formula
Tones of greyed dark green**

light   medium   dark

Refer to page 30 for tones of greyed dark green and mix according to the directions.

1 Study the painting on page 33.
2 Paint the dark side of the house with dark tone. Paint a few strokes of purple over it, then with clean knife scratch in an impression of a window.
3 Paint the roof edge, the chimney and the little shed on the left with dark tone.
4 Paint an impression of a doorway in the shed with purple, then add a touch of alizarin crimson above it.
5 With light sky tone paint the top part of the roof, the front of the house, the little extension and the left side of the shed.
6 Paint the side of the extension and an impression of a doorway with purple.

FENCE
1 Study the painting on page 33.
2 Paint a mixture of dark greyed dark green tone and purple on fence, using up and down strokes.
3 Paint a few strokes of extra light sky tone on fence near house.
4 Paint a few strokes of purple on right corner of fence and add a few touches of alizarin crimson.
5 Using the corner of knife, score the fence with up and down strokes, finishing with two horizontal strokes.

ROAD

Colour tone
to $\frac{1}{2}$ **teaspoon extra light sky tone**
add $\frac{1}{2}$ **teaspoon light greyed dark green tone**
       $\frac{1}{4}$ **teaspoon yellow ochre**

1 Study the painting on page 33.
2 Paint the road with the tone just mixed, using strokes that go straight across.
3 On the lower half of the road paint strokes of medium greyed dark green tone. Add a few strokes of dark sky tone over the light tone as indicated.
4 Paint an uneven curved line down centre of road with dark greyed dark green tone and add a few touches of purple. Paint light tone on right side of the line for highlight.

GROUND
1 Study the painting on page 33.
2 Paint the top lefthand side between the rocks with light greyed dark green tone.
3 Paint medium tone in the middle and dark tone alternately with purple across the bottom of the canvas where indicated. Take care to retain texture.
4 In this same bottom area, paint dark sky tones and add a few touches of alizarin crimson. Paint an uneven purple line along edge of road.
5 Paint the ground along fence in exactly the same way.

ROCKS
1 Study the painting on page 33.
2 Paint the left, the top and bottom of rocks with a mixture of dark greyed dark green tones and purple.
3 Paint purple on ground underneath rocks, for shadows.
4 Paint dark greyed dark green tone on right side and bottom of rocks along fence.
5 On the rocks near the trees and on the left side of the rocks near the fence paint extra light sky tone, for highlight.
6 Paint a few highlights on other rocks where indicated with medium sky tone.

TREES

1 Study the painting on page 33.
2 Paint tree trunks with medium round brush and purple. Then paint over trunks with knife, for texture.
3 Paint branches blowing to the right with medium round brush and purple. Then, with clean knife, scratch out the ends of the branches to give a delicate, wispy look.
4 With clean knife scratch in wet paint a feeling of wild grasses and shrub between the rocks.
5 Paint a few flying birds with purple. No eagles please — they should be delicate.
6 Finish with a few touches of aqua on tree trunks, branches, ground, shed and fence.

This is an unusual painting with a brooding, dramatic quality. You will love it.

Yellow Shrub Roses

THE DRAWING

1 Use canvas board, canvas or hardboard, 14 in. (36cm) by 18 in. (46cm) vertically.
2 Study the drawing and painting on pages 38 and 39.
3 Arrange the palette according to the palette layout on page 8.
4 Use the large, flat hog brush to stain the canvas with a light wash of burnt umber, as described in Step 1 on page 7. Wipe with toilet tissue.
5 With the medium round brush and dark umber wash put in the grid lines and simple drawing as indicated on page 38. Notice positions of flowers.
6 The light is coming from the left and top, so with dark umber wash lightly shade in areas of flowers as indicated.
7 Clean your brushes in the medium of turpentine or white spirit.

THE PAINTING

BACKGROUND (slight variation from other backgrounds)

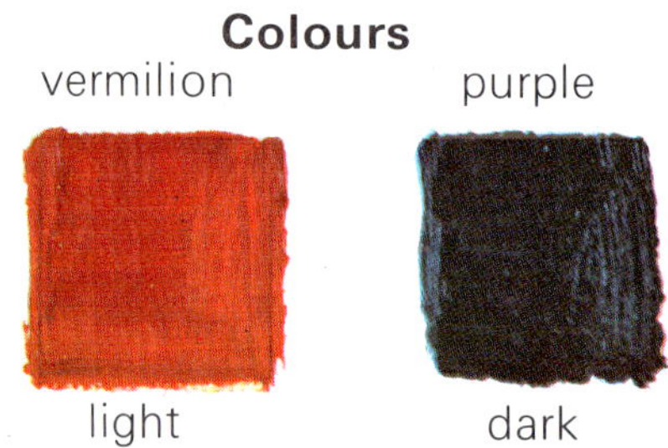

The above colours are used from the palette and require no mixing.

Let's paint

Use offset knife, held lightly.

1 Study the painting on page 39.

2 Paint the entire background with purple, using flat of the knife. Go between petals of
   roses but paint out leaves and stems for now.
3 Paint vermilion over purple lightly here and there where indicated, slanting strokes
   towards centre of flowers. Do not load the knife with paint.
4 With clean knife scratch the stems and leaves in wet paint.

ROSES

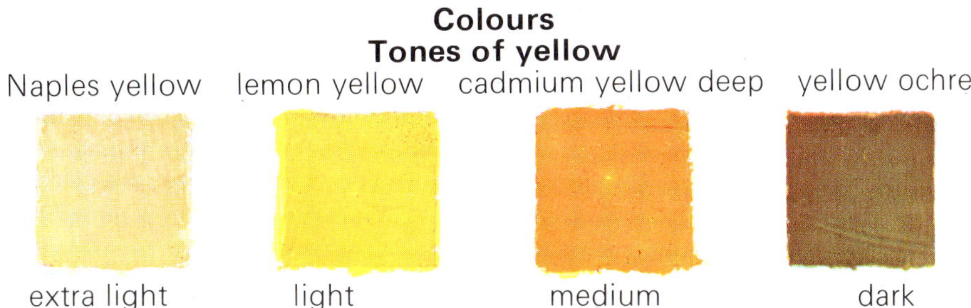

**Colours
Tones of yellow**

Naples yellow	lemon yellow	cadmium yellow deep	yellow ochre
extra light	light	medium	dark

The above colours are used from the palette and require no mixing.

1 Study the painting on page 39.
2 Paint the top petals of the two upper roses with extra light and light tones. Paint light
   tone around stamens, then tip petals with extra light tone. Put a few touches of
   medium tone on right petals of both roses. (They are in semi-profile.)
3 Paint the shaded area of the rose petals in front of each bloom with medium tone on
   the left and dark tone on the right. Use flat of the knife and slant strokes towards the
   centre. Keep petals rounded at the bottom.
4 Paint the centre rose mostly with extra light and light tones. Keep medium tone
   emanating from stamen area and fading to the light and extra light tones. Retain the
   loose feeling of the petals by scratching with knife around edges of petals.
5 Paint the top petals of the two roses at the bottom of the canvas with extra light tone.
   Shade the edges of the petals with light and medium tones, using mostly medium tone
   on the right petals.
6 Paint the shaded area of the petals on the left bloom with medium tone, then add a
   touch of dark tone. Paint the shaded petals of the other rose with dark tone only. The
   stamens will be painted later.

LEAVES, STEMS AND BUDS

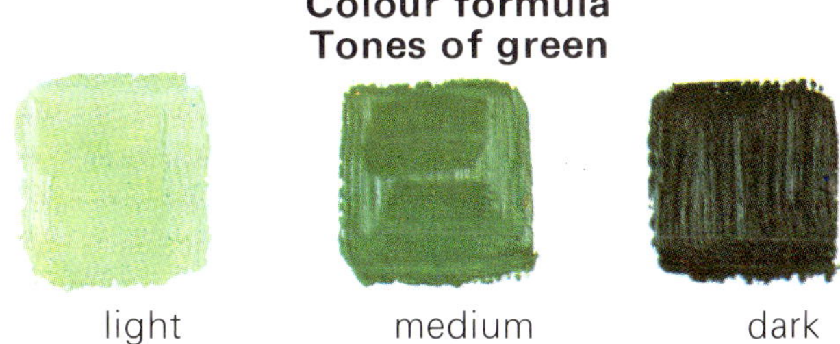

**Colour formula
Tones of green**

light	medium	dark

Refer to page 14 for tones of green and mix according to the directions. You will also
need an additional tone which you mix in the following way:

Extra light tone
to ¼ **teaspoon light green tone**
add ½ **teaspoon lemon yellow**

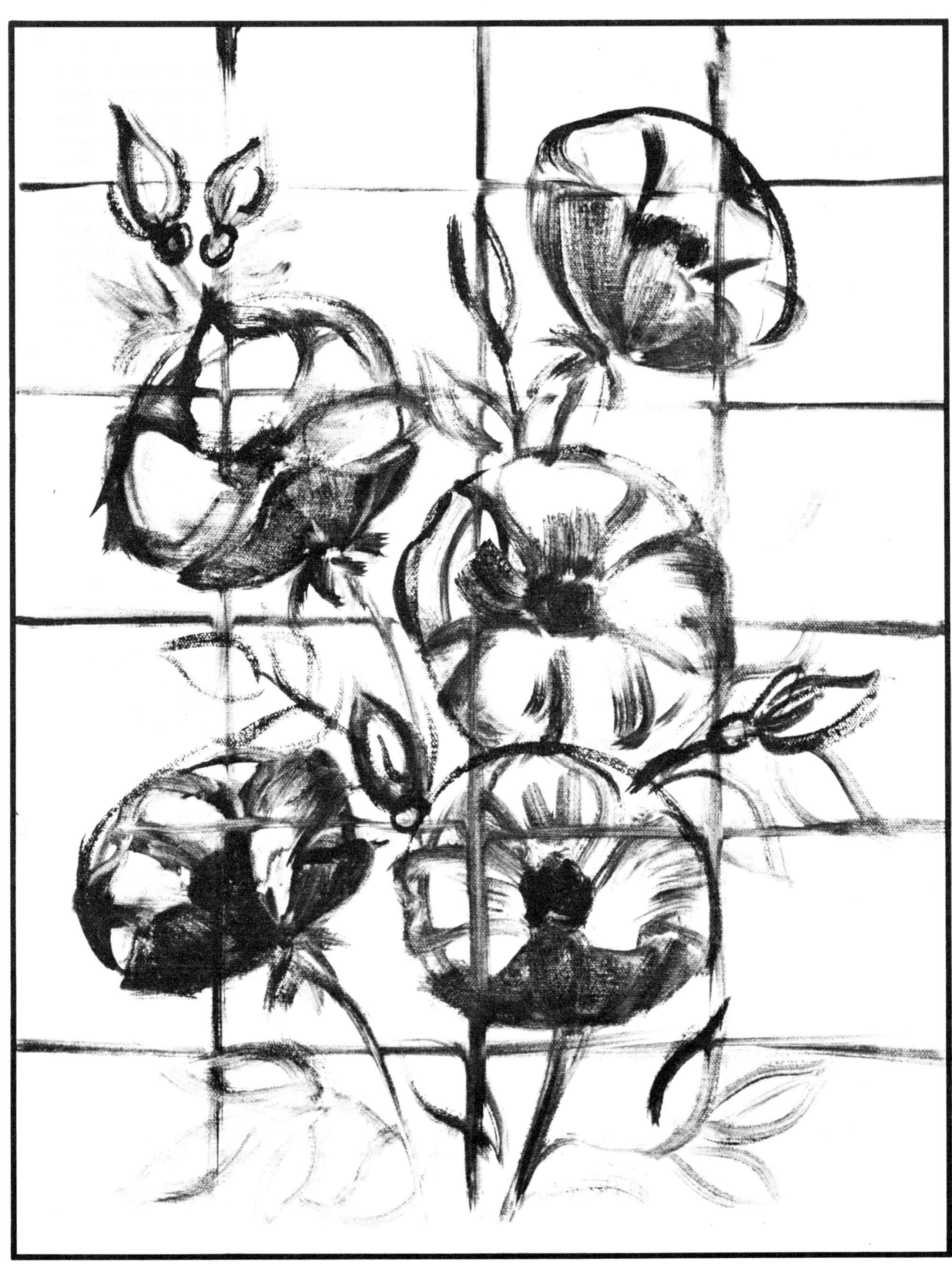

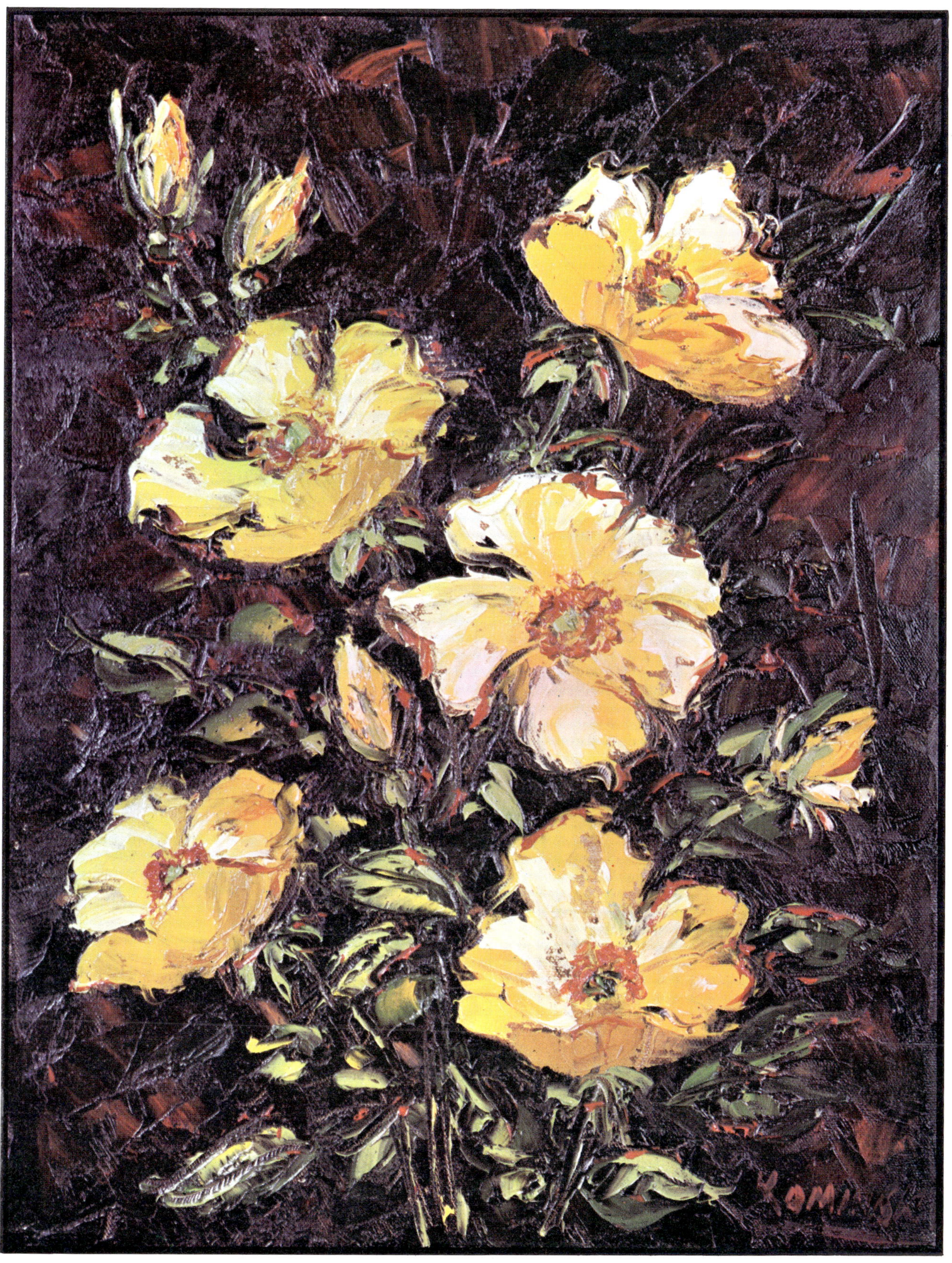

1 Study the painting on the previous page.
2 Paint leaves on right side of blooms with mostly medium and dark tones. Use flat of knife and make sure they are not too large.
3 Paint leaves in the centre and left of canvas with medium, light and extra light tones.
4 Paint short leaves under flowers with medium tone on right side, and light and extra light tones on the left side.
5 Paint leaves around the buds with medium and light tones and tip them with light and medium yellow tones, and a touch of alizarin crimson.
6 Paint a blob of light green tone in the centre of each rose, then stipple in the stamens with vermilion. Add a few touches of alizarin crimson on the stamens on the right side.
7 Paint a delicate line of vermilion around rose petals and on leaves where indicated.
8 Finish with a few touches of medium yellow tone on the stems and leaves.

I feel certain you enjoyed the brilliant contrasts of colour in this painting.

Still Life with Fish

THE DRAWING

1 Use canvas board, canvas or hardboard, 14 in. (36cm) by 18 in. (46cm) horizontally.
2 Study the drawing and painting on pages 42 and 43.
3 Arrange the palette according to the palette layout on page 8.
4 Use the large, flat hog brush to stain the canvas with a light wash of burnt umber, as described in Step 1 on page 7. Wipe with toilet tissue.
5 With the medium round brush and dark umber wash put in the grid lines and simple drawing as indicated on page 42. Notice the angle of the fish on the canvas and the cloth beneath it.
6 The light is coming from the left, so with dark umber wash lightly shade the right areas of the drawing where indicated.
7 Clean your brushes in the medium of turpentine or white spirit.

THE PAINTING

BACKGROUND (similar to the previous painting of Yellow Shrub Roses)

Colours

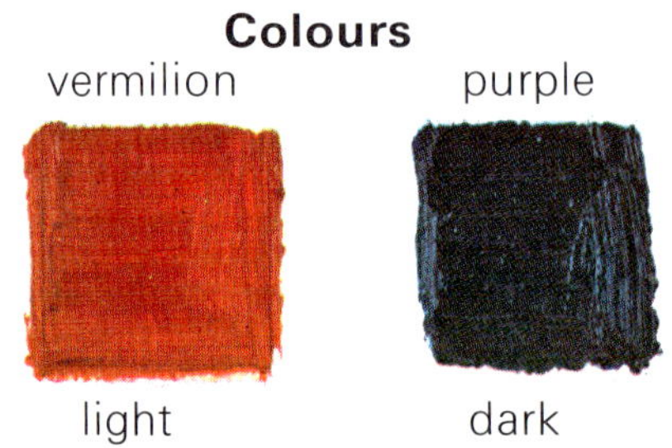

The above colours are used from the palette and require no mixing.

Let's paint
Use offset knife, held lightly.

1 Study the painting on page 43.
2 Paint the entire background and the two lower corners with purple. Use long, flowing strokes. Paint out basil leaves (in blue pot) and parsley for now.
3 Paint long, flowing strokes of vermilion on left and middle of canvas. Paint some in the lower corners and a little on the right of canvas.

ORANGE JAR

Colour formula
Tones of burnt orange

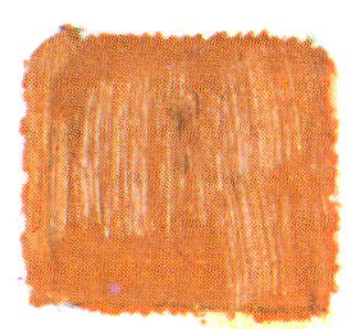 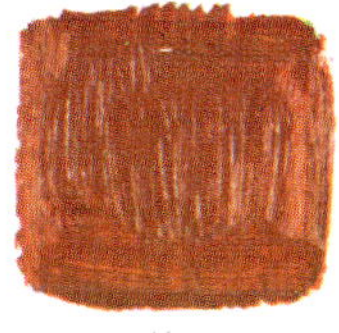 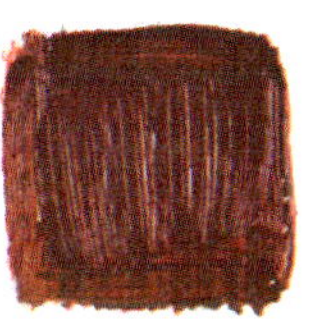

light   medium   dark

Medium tone
1 tablespoon orange
½ teaspoon vermilion
¼ teaspoon purple
Mix and separate into three parts, one small (½ teaspoon) and two equal parts.
First part (½ teaspoon) for light tone
add   ½ teaspoon white
½ teaspoon orange
¼ teaspoon cadmium yellow deep

Second part for medium tone: do not touch

Third part for dark tone
add   ¼ teaspoon purple
¼ teaspoon alizarin crimson

Clean your knife.

1 Study the painting on page 43.
2 Paint right side of jar with dark tone. Watch the form and shape of the lip.
3 Paint medium tone in centre of jar and light tone on left side. Blend lightly.
4 Outline the entire lip and right side of jar with purple.
5 Paint a line of dark tone across centre of jar curved downwards following the shape of the lip. (The cork and highlights will be painted in later.)

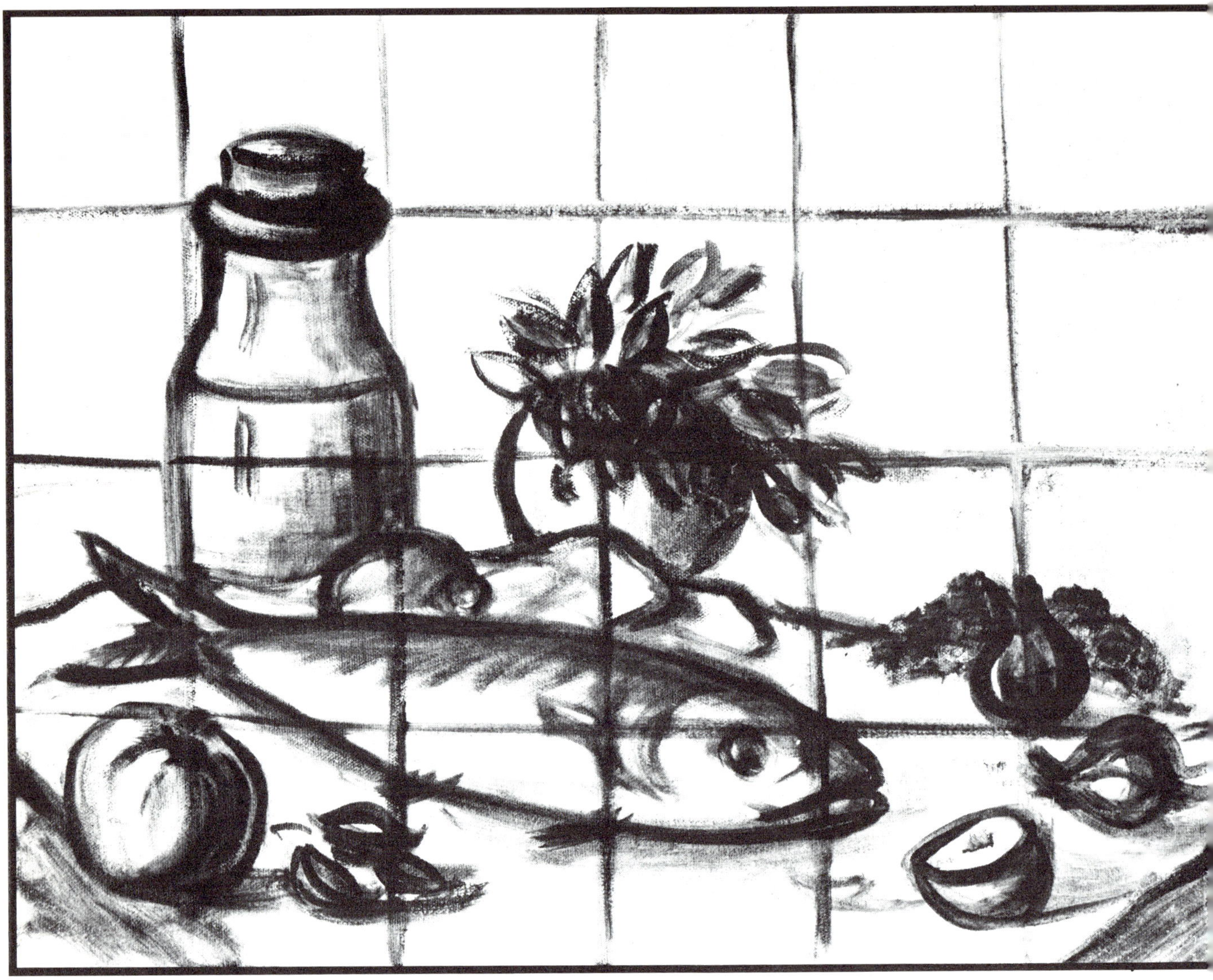

WHITE CLOTH

The following colour tones are used for both the cloth and the fish.

**Colour formula
Tones of white**

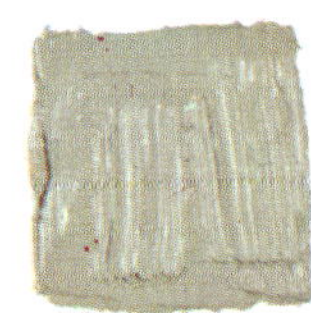

light   medium   dark

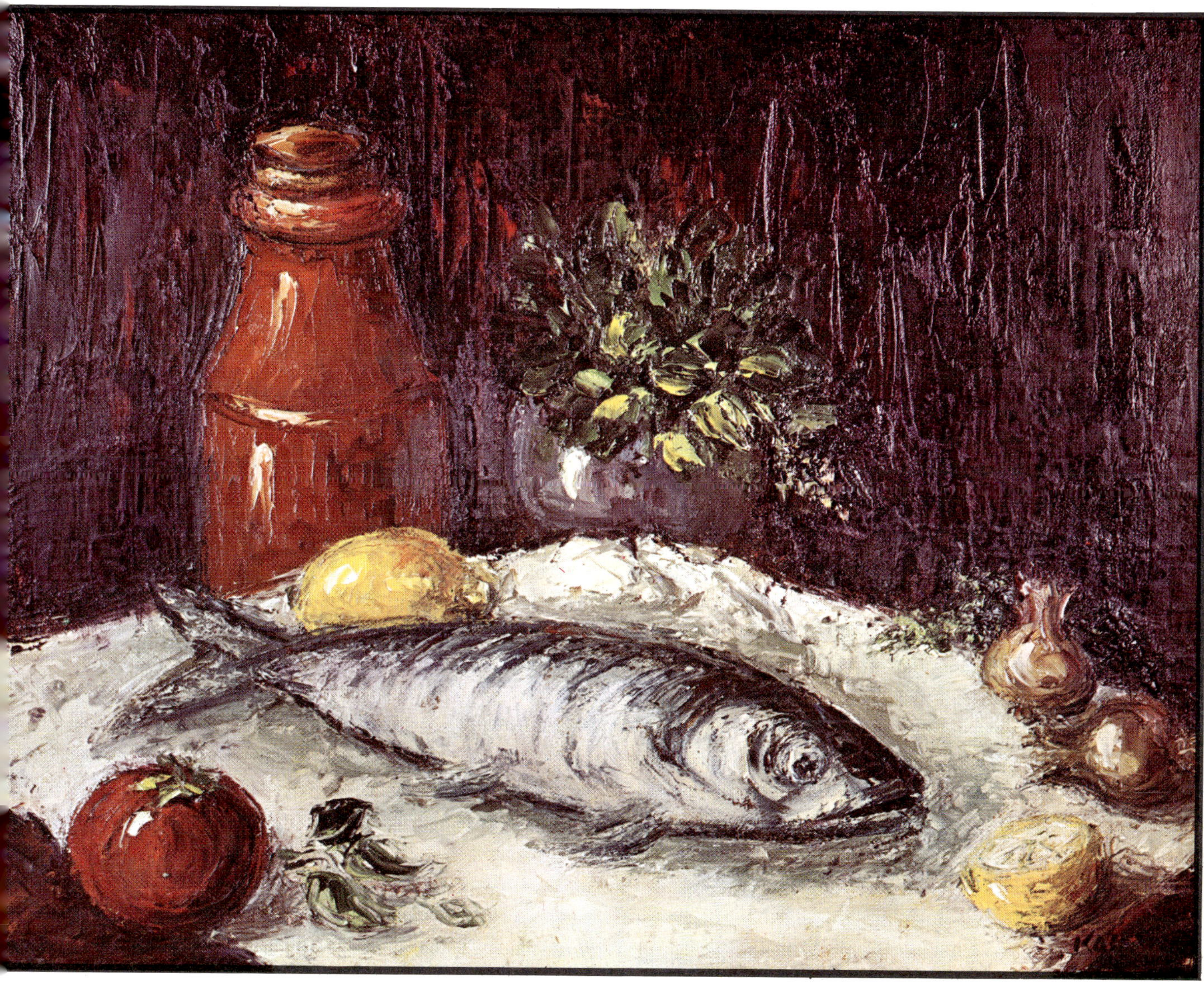

The procedure for mixing this colour is different from the previous methods.

Light tone
1¾ **tablespoons white**
¼ **teaspoon Naples yellow**
Mix and separate into three equal parts
First part for light tone: do not touch

Second part for medium tone
add   ⅛ **teaspoon burnt umber**
⅛ **teaspoon aqua**

Third part for dark tone
add   ¼ **teaspoon burnt umber**
¼ **teaspoon aqua**
⅛ **teaspoon yellow ochre**

1 Study the painting on the previous page.
2 Paint dark tone in the folds and around the fish, using flat of knife.
3 Paint medium tone next to the dark tone in the foreground around the fish.
4 Paint light tone on the rest of the cloth. Use flat strokes slanting to the left in the foreground.
5 Blend the dark, medium and light tones, taking care not to lose tonal values.
6 Paint shadows under the tomato, the cut lemon and onions with dark tone.

FISH (no sharks please!)
In addition to the tones of white mixed for the cloth, you will need a blue tone which you mix in the following way:

Blue tone

to $\frac{3}{4}$ **teaspoon dark white tone**
add $\frac{1}{8}$ **teaspoon blue**

1 Study the painting on the previous page.
2 Starting at the head, paint the top of the fish with dark white tone, using curved strokes going halfway across it.
3 Paint the tail with dark white tone.
4 Paint the other half of the fish with medium white tone. Add a few strokes of dark tone where indicated.
5 With blue tone paint the markings across the top, using half-round strokes.
6 Paint the eye and area around eye with the same blue tone.
7 Outline the whole of the fish including the tail with a mixture of $\frac{1}{2}$ teaspoon burnt umber and $\frac{1}{2}$ teaspoon blue. With the same mixture shade the top of the head and accent the mouth and the fins lying on the cloth.
8 Paint short, curved strokes of light white tone in the middle of the body, for highlight.

BLUE POT
1 Study the painting on the previous page.
2 Paint the blue pot with the blue tone mixed for the fish.
3 Paint purple on right side of pot, for shadow. The highlight will be added later.

TOMATO

Colours
Tones of red

cadmium orange	vermilion	alizarin crimson

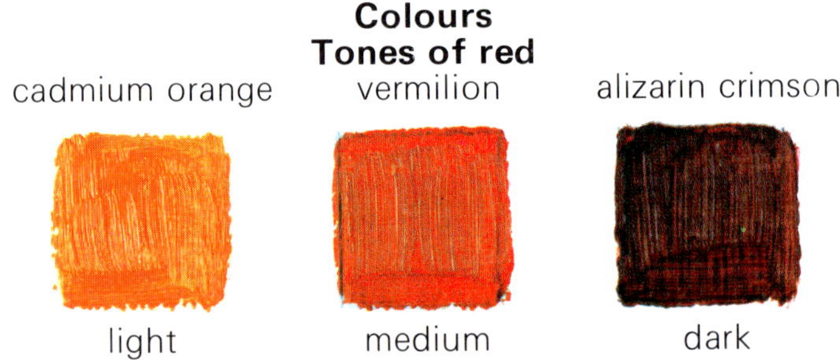

light	medium	dark

The above colours are used from the palette and require no mixing.

1 Study the painting on the previous page. Use round strokes to paint the tomato.
2 Paint right side and bottom of tomato with dark tone.
3 Paint medium tone in the middle and light tone on the left.
4 Blend all tones lightly. (The stalk and highlight will be added later.)

BASIL AND PARSLEY

Colour formula
Tones of green

light   medium   dark

Refer to page 14 for tones of green and mix according to the directions.

1 Study the painting on page 43.
2 Paint basil leaves in the background with dark tone.
3 Paint leaves in the foreground with medium tone, then add touches of light tone.
4 Paint leaves near the tomato with dark and light tones.
5 Paint the green stalk of the tomato with medium tone on the right and light tone on the left.
6 Using stippling strokes paint the parsley with dark tone on the right and light and medium tones on the left.

ONIONS AND CORK

Colour formula
Tones of beige

light   medium   dark

Medium tone
1 teaspoon yellow ochre
$\frac{1}{8}$ teaspoon purple
Mix and separate into three parts, one small ($\frac{1}{2}$ teaspoon) and two equal parts.
First part ($\frac{1}{2}$ teaspoon) for light tone
add $\frac{3}{4}$ teaspoon white
$\frac{1}{2}$ teaspoon cadmium yellow deep
$\frac{1}{8}$ teaspoon orange

Second part for medium tone: do not touch

Third part for dark tone
add $\frac{1}{8}$ teaspoon purple
touch of orange

1 Study the painting on page 43.
2 Paint dark tone on the right side and bottom of onions, using round strokes.
3 Paint medium tone in the middle.
4 Paint light tone on left side.
5 With tip of knife drag up dark and light tones to create a tassel effect at the top. Add a few at the bottom of the onions, in the same way.

6 Paint a few touches of cadmium orange on the onions where indicated.
7 Paint the cork with dark tone. Highlight it with light tone and outline it with purple.

LEMONS

Colours
Tones of yellow

Naples yellow   lemon yellow   cadmium yellow deep   yellow ochre

extra light   light   medium   dark

The above colours are used from the palette and require no mixing.

1 Study the painting on page 43.
2 Paint dark tone on right side of lemons, medium tone in the centre and light tone on
   the left.
3 Paint inside of cut lemon with extra light tone, then score it with clean knife.
4 Add a few touches of cadmium orange on the lemon skins.

HIGHLIGHTS

Colour tone
$\frac{1}{2}$ teaspoon white
$\frac{1}{4}$ teaspoon Naples yellow

1 Paint highlights of the above tone on orange jar, blue pot, tomato, onions and lemons,
   using short, curved strokes in the shape of the objects.
2 Paint touches of lemon yellow on the basil leaves in the foreground of the blue pot.

I am sure this was an enjoyable painting – even if the fish was a bit difficult. It can only
get easier.

Early Spring

THE DRAWING
1 Use canvas board, canvas or hardboard, 14 in. (36cm) by 18 in. (46cm) vertically.
2 Study the drawing and painting on pages 48 and 49.
3 Arrange the palette according to the palette layout on page 8.
4 Use the large, flat hog brush to stain the canvas with a light wash of burnt umber, as described in Step 1 on page 7. Wipe with toilet tissue.
5 With the medium round brush and dark umber wash put in the grid lines and simple drawing as indicated on page 48. Draw only the large tree trunk for now. You can put in the branches later.
6 The light is coming from the right, so with dark umber wash lightly shade in the left side of hills, tree trunk, water and under daffodils.
7 Clean your brushes in the medium of turpentine or white spirit.

THE PAINTING

SKY

**Colour formula
Sky tones**

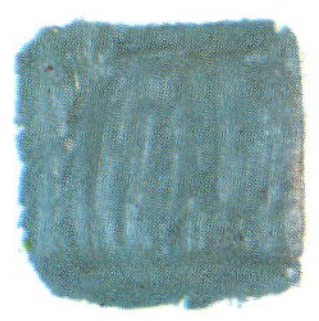

light   medium   dark

Refer to page 22 for sky tones and mix according to the directions. Only the light and medium tones are used for the sky. The dark tone will be used for the hills. You will also need an additional tone which you mix in the following way:

Extra light tone
$\frac{1}{2}$ **teaspoon white**
$\frac{1}{2}$ **teaspoon Naples yellow**

Clean your knife.

Let's paint
Use offset knife, held lightly.

1 Study the painting on page 49.
2 Paint light tone around top of hills and halfway up into the sky.
3 Starting at the top of the canvas, paint medium tone and work into the light tone.
4 Paint extra light tone over the hills and blend lightly into the light tone.

HILLS
1 Study the painting on page 49.
2 Paint dark sky tone on left side of the hills.
3 For the pale tones of the hills, mix the remaining light sky tone with $\frac{1}{8}$ teaspoon purple. Paint right side of hills with this tone and dark tone alternately.
4 Paint purple at the base of the hills along the water.
5 Lightly drag the sky colour over the hills to soften the outline. (The light green tone will be added later.)

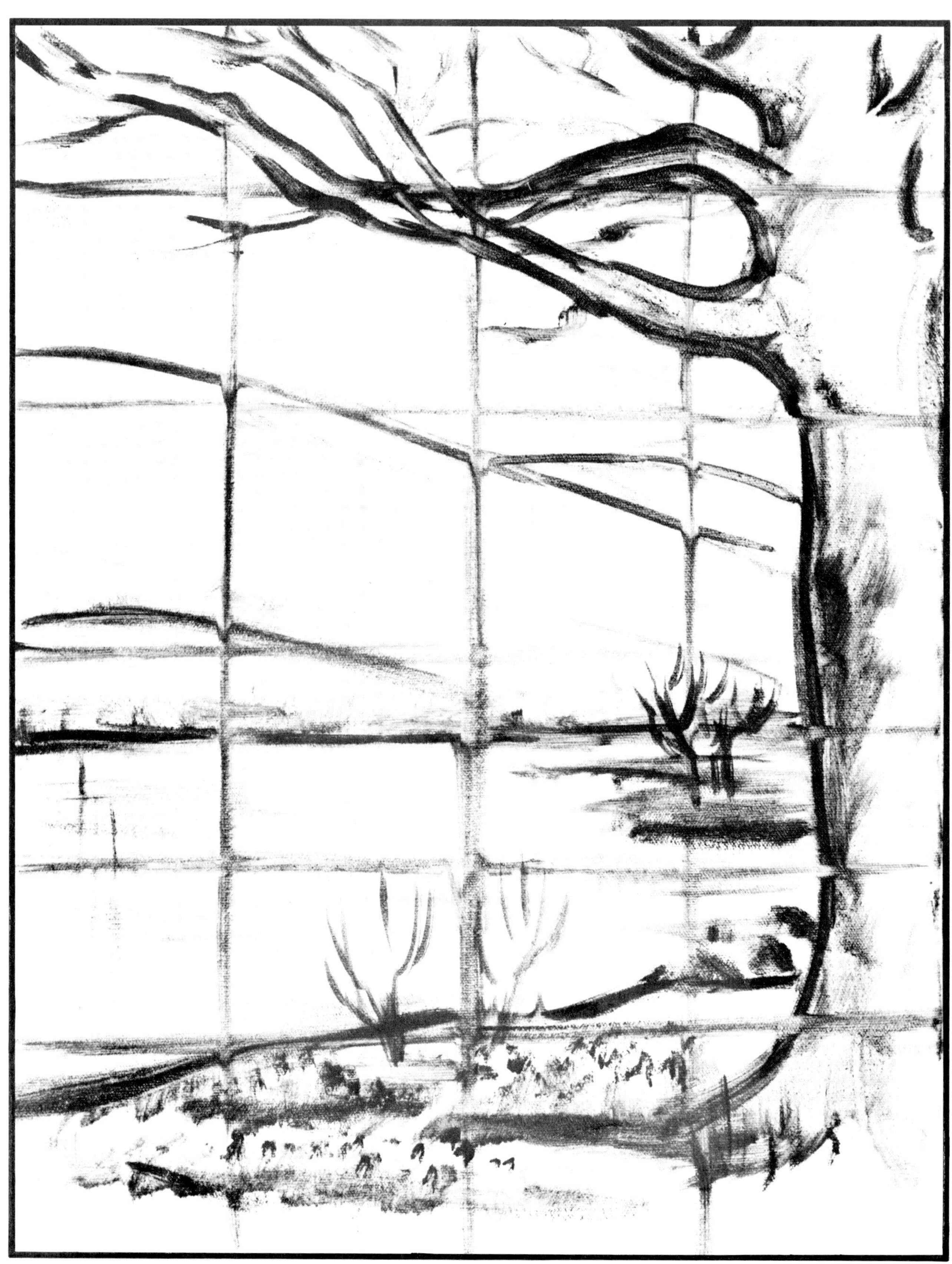

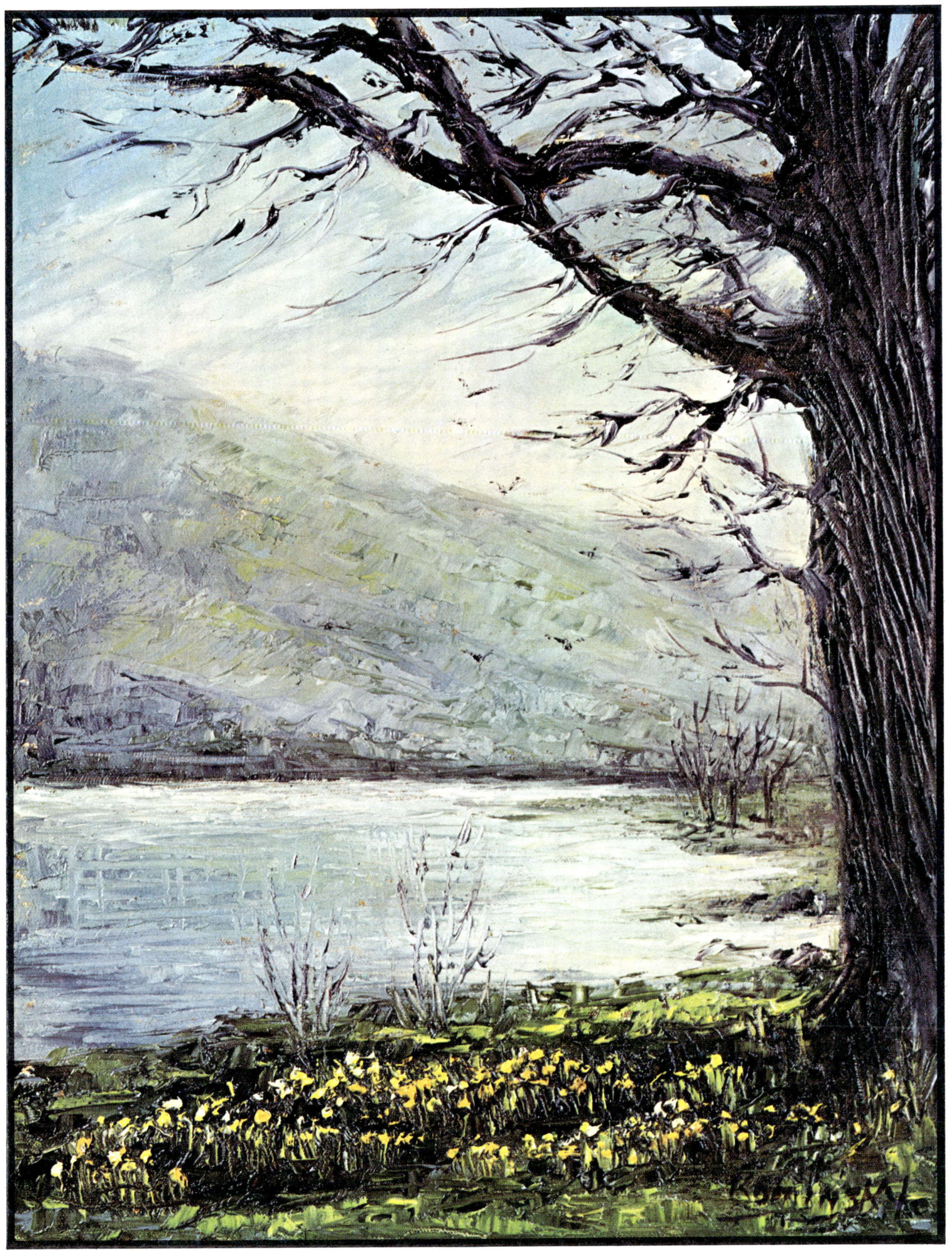

WATER

As the colours of the water reflect those of the sky, you will need the same sky tones.
Mix another batch according to the directions on page 22. You will also need an additional tone which you mix in the following way:

Extra light tone
$\frac{1}{2}$ teaspoon white
$\frac{1}{4}$ teaspoon Naples yellow

1 Study the painting on the previous page.
2 Paint light tone along the base of the hills and on the right of the water down to the shoreline.
3 Paint dark tone on the left of the water.
4 Paint medium tone in centre of water and gradually blend it in with the light and dark tones.
5 For the sparkle paint extra light tone on the right of the water and along the edge of the hills.

GRASS

Colour formula
Tones of green

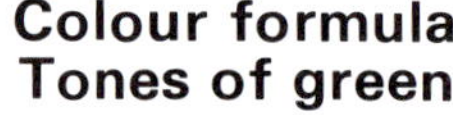

light   medium   dark

Refer to page 14 for tones of green and mix according to the directions.

1 Study the painting on the previous page.
2 Paint dark tone in front of the tree and under flowers.
3 Paint alternate strokes of light and medium tones for grass along water's edge and in the foreground.
4 Paint light tone for the grass on the right.
5 Paint the stems of daffodils with light tone but do not lose the dark tones of the shadows underneath.
6 Paint the small area of land on the right of the water with light tone.
7 Paint a few rocks on this area of land with purple and light sky tone. Keep them indistinct.
8 Paint light green tone over the hills where indicated.

TREE

This dominates the painting.

1 Study the painting on the previous page.
2 Paint the trunk with purple. Notice the texture of the trunk and paint with long, flowing strokes.
3 Paint the heavy branches with purple.
4 With medium round brush paint the lighter branches with purple. Keep them slender and delicate.
5 Paint the right side of trunk with dark sky tone to give highlights.

6 Blend base of tree into shadows of grass.
7 Paint the two bare bushes in the foreground and the small trees on the right with purple. Make them very delicate.
8 Paint a few flying birds with purple.

DAFFODILS

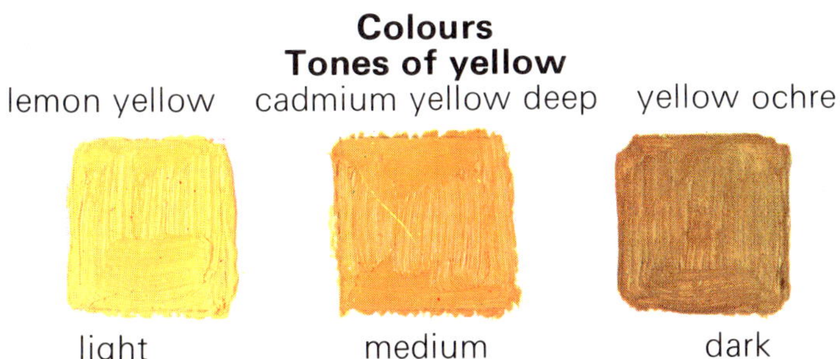

Colours
Tones of yellow

lemon yellow   cadmium yellow deep   yellow ochre

light   medium   dark

The above colours are used from the palette and require no mixing.

1 Study the painting on page 49.
2 Paint small blobs on the stems with alternate light, medium and dark tones. Use the light tone mostly at the top. Keep the flowers in uneven masses to give just an impression.

In this painting you have captured the first magical moment of spring.

Lilacs

THE DRAWING
1 Use canvas board, canvas or hardboard, 14 in. (36cm) by 18 in. (46cm) horizontally.
2 Study the drawing and painting on pages 54 and 55.
3 Arrange the palette according to the palette layout on page 8.
4 Use the large, flat hog brush to stain the canvas with a light wash of burnt umber, as described in Step 1 on page 7. Wipe with toilet tissue.
5 With the medium round brush and dark umber wash put in the grid lines and simple drawing as indicated on page 54. Draw the flowers in uneven cones.
6 The light is coming from the top, so with dark umber wash lightly shade flowers where indicated.
7 Clean your brushes in the medium of turpentine or white spirit.

THE PAINTING

BACKGROUND

**Colour formula
Tones of greyed light green**

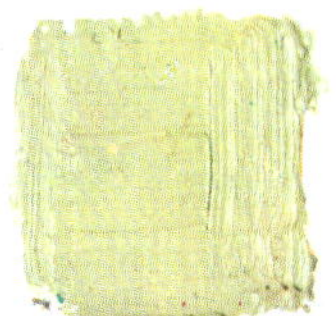  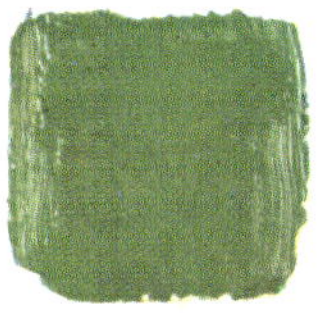

light   medium   dark

Refer to page 10 for tones of greyed light green and mix according to the directions.

Let's paint
Use offset knife, held lightly.

1 Study the painting on page 55.
2 Paint in the background starting with light tone at the top. Use long, downward strokes.
3 Paint downward strokes of medium tone on left and right side of canvas, going into the flowers a little. Paint out yellow flowers and leaves for now.
4 Paint dark tone over the bottom of the canvas, again with long, downward strokes. Blend tones lightly.
5 Paint downward strokes of purple under bowl for shadows, then with clean knife score the canvas horizontally over this to make reflections.
6 Paint a few downward strokes of purple at the top and sides of canvas.

VASE

**Colour formula
Tones of blue**

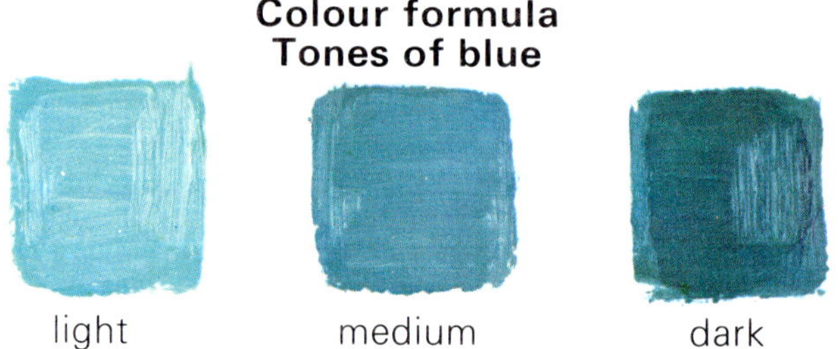

light   medium   dark

Refer to page 15 for tones of blue and mix according to the directions.

1 Study the painting on page 55.
2 Paint dark tone on right side and bottom of vase.
3 Paint medium tone in the middle and light tone on the left side of vase. Blend tones lightly. Highlights will be added later.
4 Lightly paint some downward strokes of light tone on right side of background.

PURPLE LILACS

Colour formula
Tones of purple

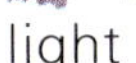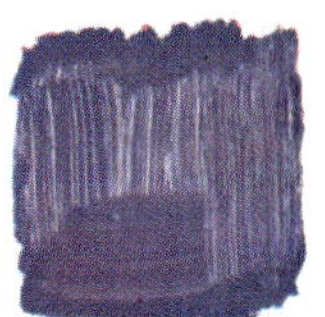

light   medium   dark

Medium tone
$\frac{3}{4}$ tablespoon white
$\frac{3}{4}$ teaspoon purple
$\frac{1}{8}$ teaspoon alizarin crimson
Mix and separate into three parts, one small ($\frac{1}{2}$ teaspoon) and two equal parts.
First part ($\frac{1}{2}$ teaspoon) for light tone
add   1 teaspoon white
    $\frac{1}{8}$ teaspoon Naples yellow
    $\frac{1}{8}$ teaspoon alizarin crimson

Second part for medium tone: do not touch

Third part for dark tone
add   1 teaspoon purple
    $\frac{1}{8}$ teaspoon alizarin crimson

Extra light tone
to $\frac{1}{2}$ teaspoon light tone
add $\frac{1}{2}$ teaspoon white
    touch of alizarin crimson
    touch of Naples yellow

1 Study the painting on page 55. Notice the cones of lilacs are not a solid mass but are uneven and are painted in three sections of colour.
2 Paint across the lower section of each cone with stippling strokes of dark tone.
3 Paint across the middle section with medium tone.
4 Paint across the top section with light tone, taking care not to lose tonal values.
5 Paint purple and alizarin crimson at base of each purple lilac, for accent.
6 Paint extra light tone here and there over the light tone, where indicated. Keep flowers loose.

WHITE LILACS

Colour formula
Tones of white

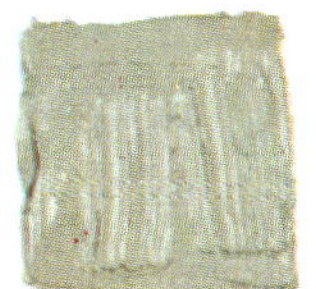

light   medium   dark

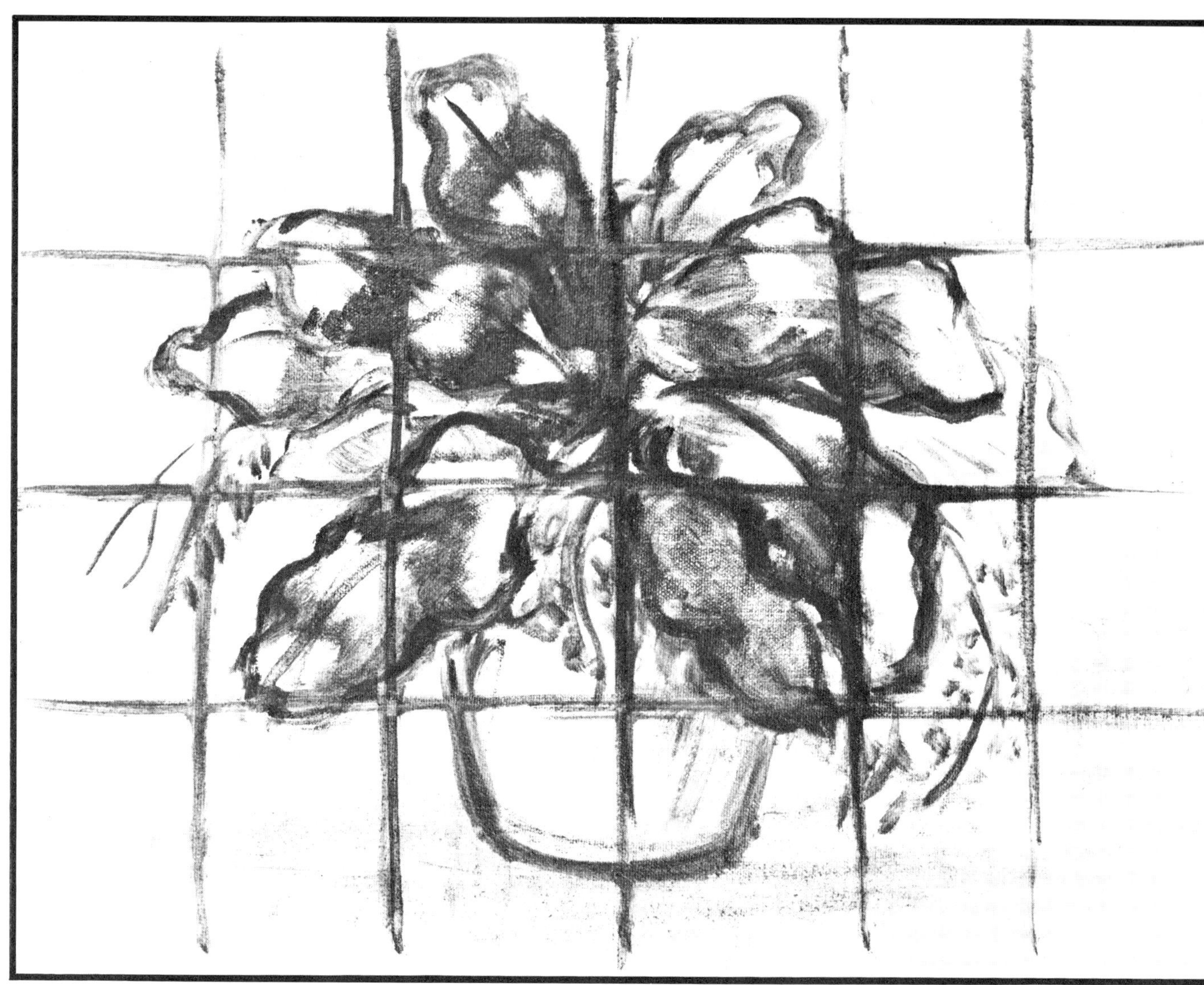

Refer to page 42 for tones of white and mix according to the directions. You will also need an additional tone which you mix in the following way:

Extra dark tone

to	$\frac{1}{4}$	**teaspoon dark tone**
add	$\frac{1}{4}$	**teaspoon burnt umber**
	$\frac{1}{4}$	**teaspoon aqua**

1 Study the painting opposite.
2 Repeat the procedure for purple lilacs. Paint dark tone across the lower section of each cone, again using stippling strokes.
3 Paint across the middle section with medium tone.
4 Paint across the top section with light tone. Keep cleaning the knife, as the white must be kept clean to be effective.
5 Keep flowers loose and paint some separate little blooms on the edges with light, medium and dark tones.

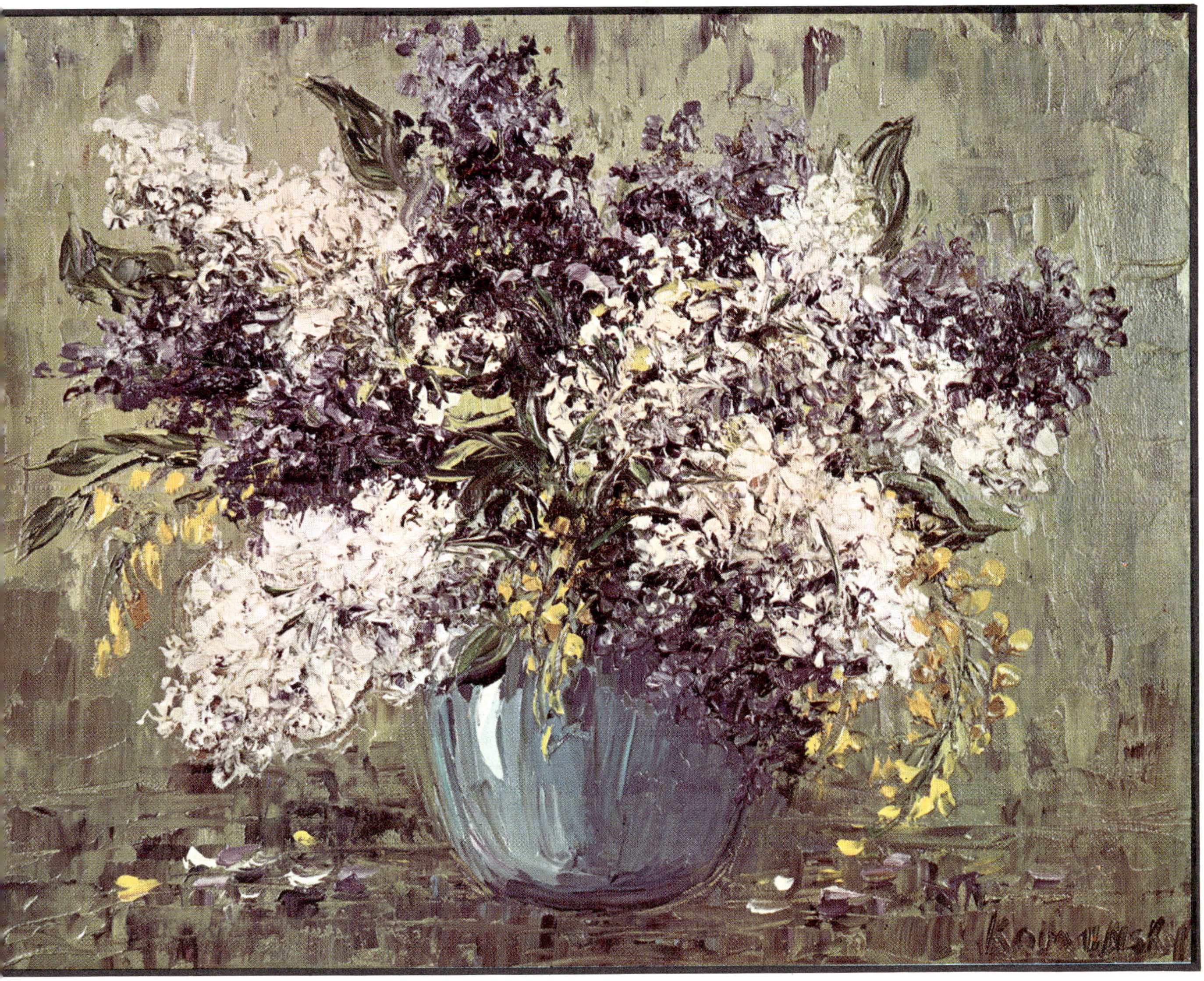

6 To accent the dark tone, stipple extra dark tone over it where indicated. Take care with the tonal values, as they are very important with the white lilacs.

LEAVES AND STEMS

**Colour formula
Tones of green**

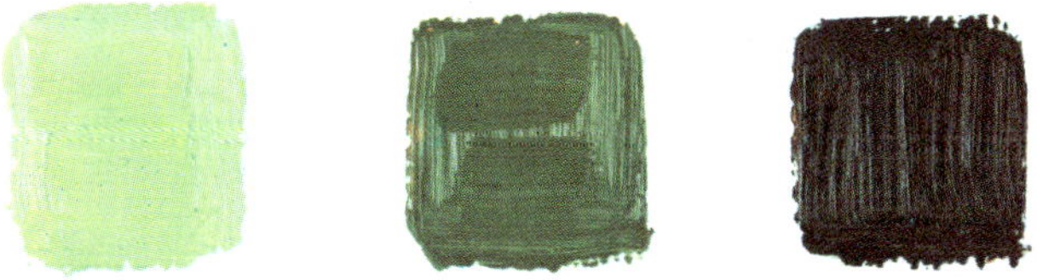

light

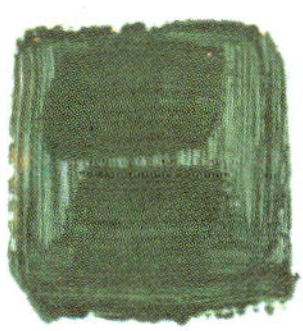

medium

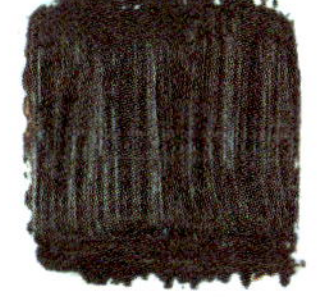

dark

Refer to page 14 for tones of green and mix according to the directions.

1 Study the painting on the previous page. There are only a few leaves and these are not very developed.
2 Paint the lilac leaves on the right of the canvas with dark and medium tones.
3 Paint the leaves in the centre and on the left of the canvas with dark tone on the right side and light tone on the left side. Do not make them very definite.
4 Paint in delicate stems for yellow flowers with light and medium tones.

YELLOW FLOWERS

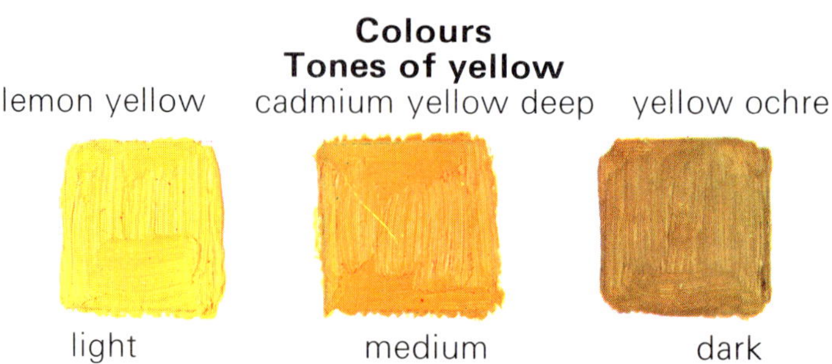

Colours
Tones of yellow

lemon yellow	cadmium yellow deep	yellow ochre
light	medium	dark

The above colours are used from the palette and require no mixing.

1 Study the painting on the previous page.
2 Paint flowers in the middle and at base of stems with medium tone.
3 Paint flowers at the end of stems with light tone.
4 Add touches of dark tone to the flowers where indicated.

HIGHLIGHTS AND FALLEN PETALS
1 Paint curved highlight on left of bowl with medium white tone.
2 Paint a few fallen petals where indicated with light and medium purple tones, light and medium yellow tones, and light white tone.
3 Paint shadows under fallen petals with purple.

In this painting the offset knife creates an effect of actual blooms.

Rain in London

THE DRAWING
1 Use canvas board, canvas or hardboard, 14 in. (36cm) by 18 in. (46cm) vertically.
2 Study the drawing and painting on pages 58 and 59.
3 Arrange the palette according to the palette layout on page 8.
4 Use the large, flat hog brush to stain the canvas with a light wash of burnt umber, as described in Step 1 on page 7. Wipe with toilet tissue.
5 With the medium round brush and dark umber wash put in the grid lines and simple drawing as indicated on page 58. Because this is a street scene, you must be careful to ensure that the drawing fits very well in the grids. Before you draw in the figure, practise first, using the following dimensions: head: $\frac{1}{2}$ in. (1.3cm) deep; shoulders to waist: 1 in. (2.5cm); waist to hem of coat: $1\frac{1}{4}$ in. (3.2cm); legs: 1 in. (2.5cm); width

of figure (shaped): approximately 1 in. (2.5cm); umbrella: $2\frac{1}{4}$ in. (5.7cm) wide and $\frac{3}{4}$ in. (2cm) deep. Draw in figure, placing it on the bottom horizontal grid line near kerb. Draw in railings last.
6 The light is coming from the sky behind buildings, so with dark umber wash lightly shade in the areas in front of objects, and the figure as indicated.
7 Clean your brushes in the medium of turpentine or white spirit.

THE PAINTING

SKY

Colour formula
Tones of greyed light green

light   medium   dark

Refer to page 10 for tones of greyed light green and mix according to the directions but doubling the quantities. You will also need an additional tone which you mix in the following way:

Extra light tone
to $\frac{1}{4}$ **teaspoon light tone**
add $\frac{3}{4}$ **teaspoon white**
$\frac{1}{8}$ **teaspoon Naples yellow**

Clean your knife.

Let's paint
Use offset knife, held lightly.

1 Study the painting on page 59.
2 Paint extra light tone around tops of buildings and up into the sky. Paint out branches and chimney pots for now.
3 Paint light tone above it, to create a stormy effect.
4 Paint dark tone at top of canvas in slanting, sweeping strokes. Take care not to lose tonal values.

BUILDINGS

In addition to the greyed light green tones you will need two tones which you mix in the following way:

A **to** $\frac{1}{4}$ **teaspoon dark greyed light green tone**
add $\frac{1}{8}$ **teaspoon orange**

B **to** $\frac{1}{4}$ **teaspoon dark greyed light green tone**
add **touch of aqua and blue**

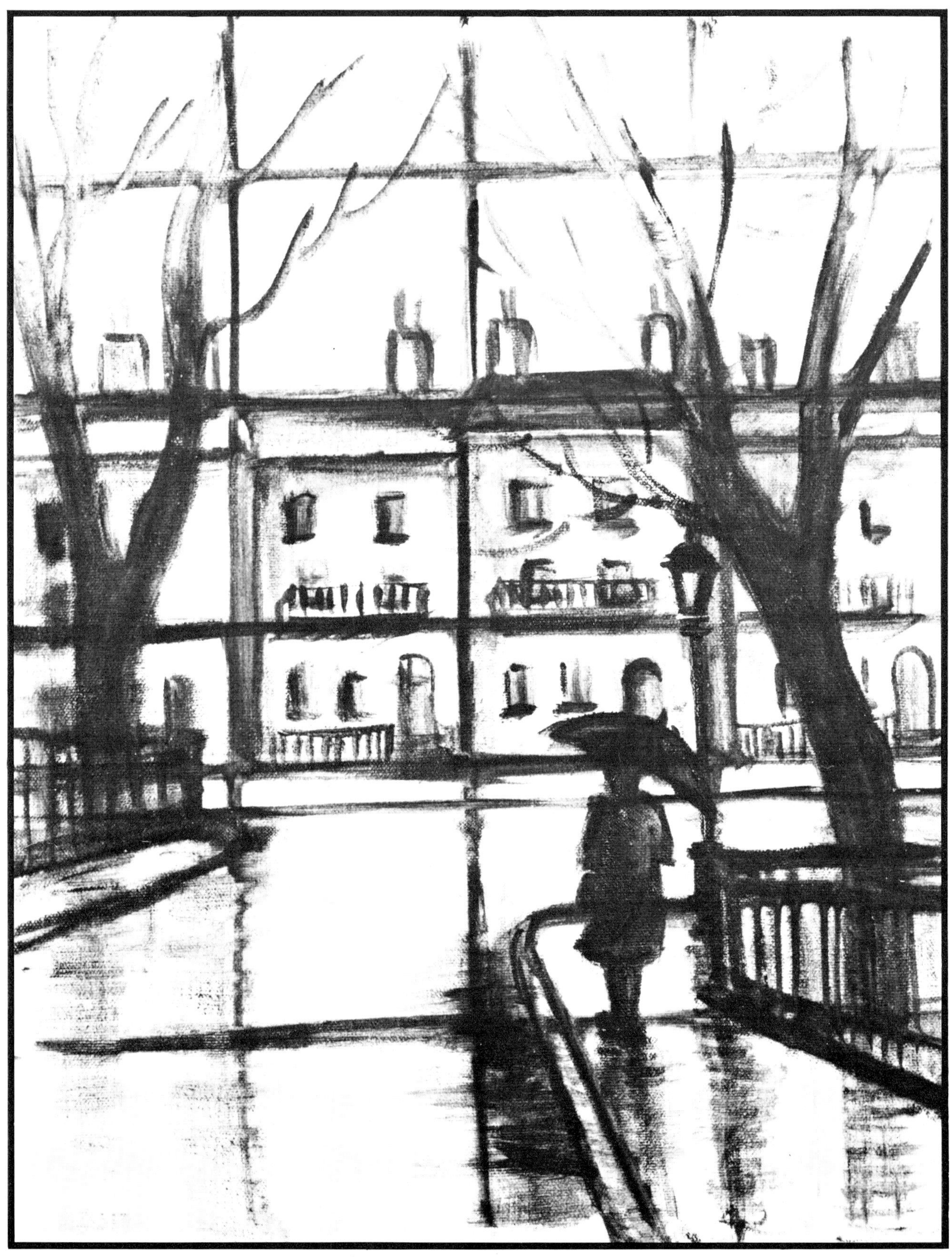

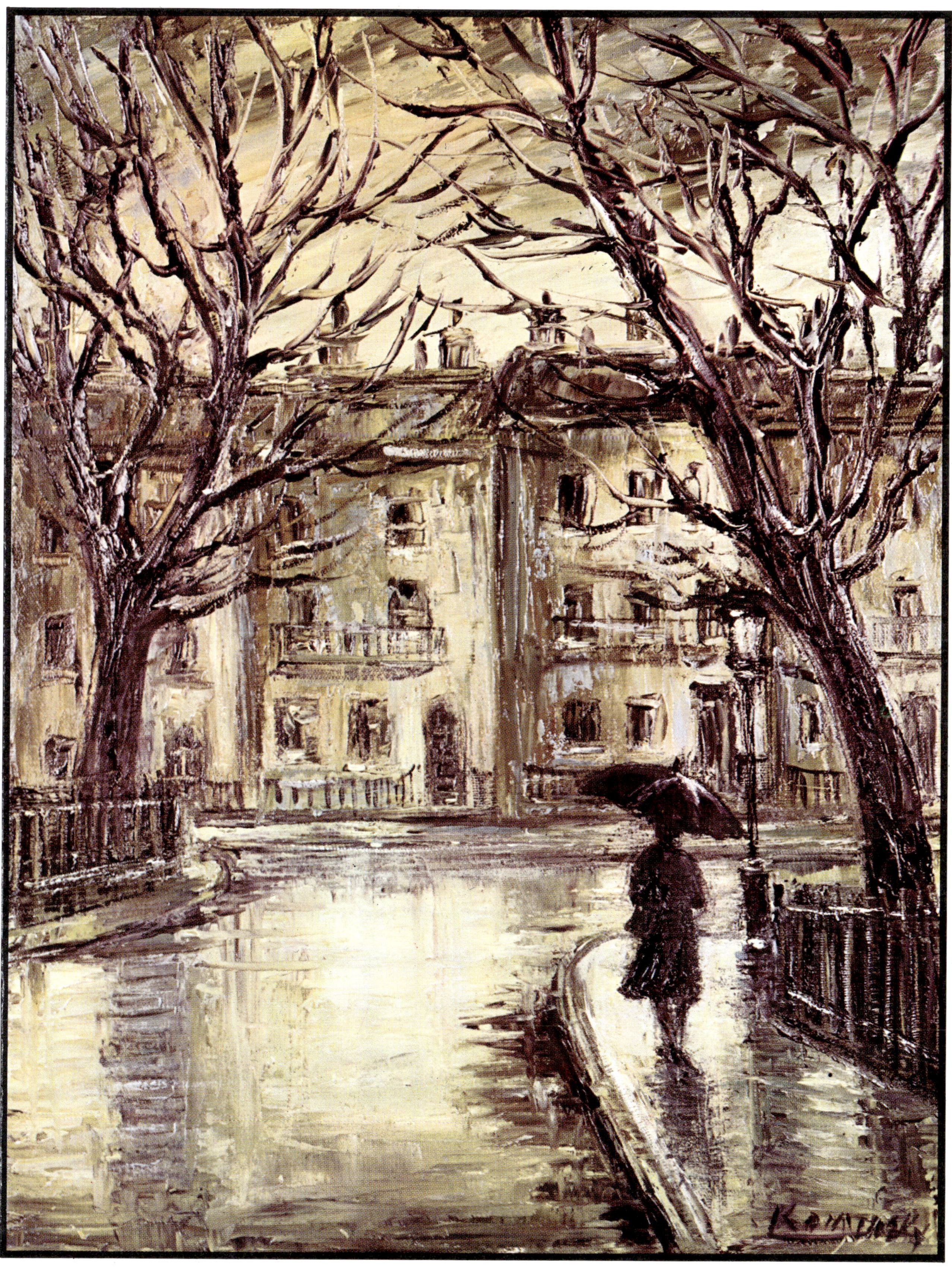

1 Study the painting on the previous page.
2 Paint tone A across roof, top and down left side of each building. Outline the roofs with purple.
3 Paint medium greyed light green tone in the middle and light tone on the right of each building.
4 Paint a few strokes of tone B on building where indicated.
5 Paint touches of tone B in the sky.

WINDOWS, DOORS AND CHIMNEY POTS

1 Study the painting on the previous page. The windows have no definite outline. Make sure they are lined up with each other.
2 Paint one stroke of purple on left side of each window and door.
3 Clean knife and finish the square or oblong by scratching the shape in wet paint.
4 Use the same technique to paint in the chimney pots.

PAVEMENTS, FENCES AND STREET

The same greyed light green tones are used again for the pavements, fences and street. However, you will also need an additional tone which you mix in the following way:

Extra dark tone
to $\frac{3}{4}$ **teaspoon dark greyed light green tone**
add $\frac{1}{8}$ **teaspoon purple**
touch of aqua

1 Study the painting on the previous page. The perspective of the pavements must be preserved.
2 Paint pavement in front of buildings with alternate light, dark, light greyed light green tones. Outline it with purple.
3 Paint right pavement with extra light tone down to feet of figure.
4 Paint medium tone to bottom of canvas.
5 Paint shadows on right pavement with extra dark tone.
6 Lightly paint strokes of extra light tone in between shadows.
7 Use extra dark tone to paint the two iron fences. Score them vertically first, then horizontally with tip of knife in wet paint to create railings.
8 Paint pavement on left first with medium tone, then dark tone.
9 Paint the street first with light tone, using long, flowing strokes going straight across the street. Paint in shadows as indicated with extra dark tone, tone B and a little purple.
10 Paint extra light tone down centre of street to give reflections of sky.
11 Paint extra dark tone across bottom of street. Blend tones lightly, taking care not to lose tonal values.
12 Accent the kerbs on both pavements with purple.
13 With clean knife put in a few light, downward strokes to give the feeling of reflections in the street.

LAMP, RAILINGS AND BALCONIES

Colour tone
$\frac{1}{4}$ **teaspoon burnt umber**
$\frac{1}{4}$ **teaspoon blue**
$\frac{1}{4}$ **teaspoon purple**

1 You may use your medium round brush if you prefer. Keep the lamp delicate and, with the above colour tone, paint it in following the drawing.
2 With the brush and same colour tone lightly paint the railings in front of the houses and on the balconies.

TREES

1 Study the painting on page 59. The tree on the right is slightly larger than the one on the left.
2 Paint both trees with purple. Use the medium round brush for the thinner branches.

FIGURE

1 Study the painting on page 59.
2 With medium round brush and purple carefully paint in the figure. Create movement in skirt as indicated.
3 Mix a little purple with medium greyed light green tone and use this colour for the legs.
4 Use a little of this same colour on right of figure and right of umbrella.

HIGHLIGHTS

1 With medium round brush paint extra light greyed light green tone on trees, railings, lamp and umbrella.

This was a very ambitious and exciting painting. If you have a storm, don't fret — just keep painting.

Breakfast Anyone?

THE DRAWING

1 Use canvas board, canvas or hardboard, 14 in. (36cm) by 18 in. (46cm) horizontally.
2 Study the drawing and painting on pages 62 and 63.
3 Arrange the palette according to the palette layout on page 8.
4 Use the large, flat hog brush to stain the canvas with a light wash of burnt umber, as described in Step 1 on page 7. Wipe with toilet tissue.
5 With the medium round brush and dark umber wash put in the grid lines and simple drawing as indicated on page 62. Make sure the eggs are oval.
6 The light is coming from the left, so with dark umber wash lightly shade objects on the right with the exception of egg shells which are hollow and therefore have the light hitting the opposite side.
7 Clean your brushes in the medium of turpentine or white spirit.

THE PAINTING

BACKGROUND

**Colour formula
Tones of yellow ochre**

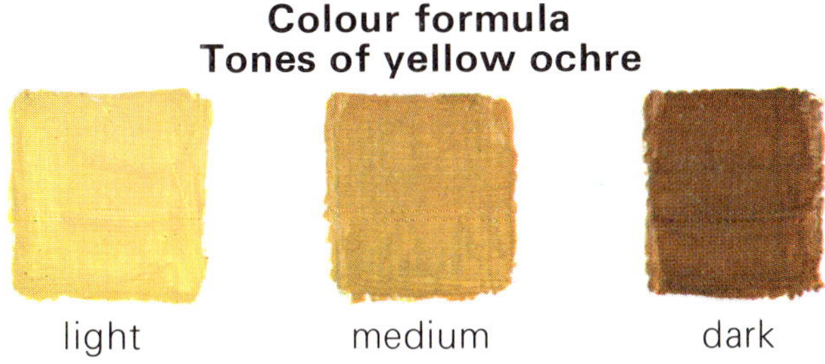

| light | medium | dark |

Refer to page 23 for tones of yellow ochre and mix according to the directions.

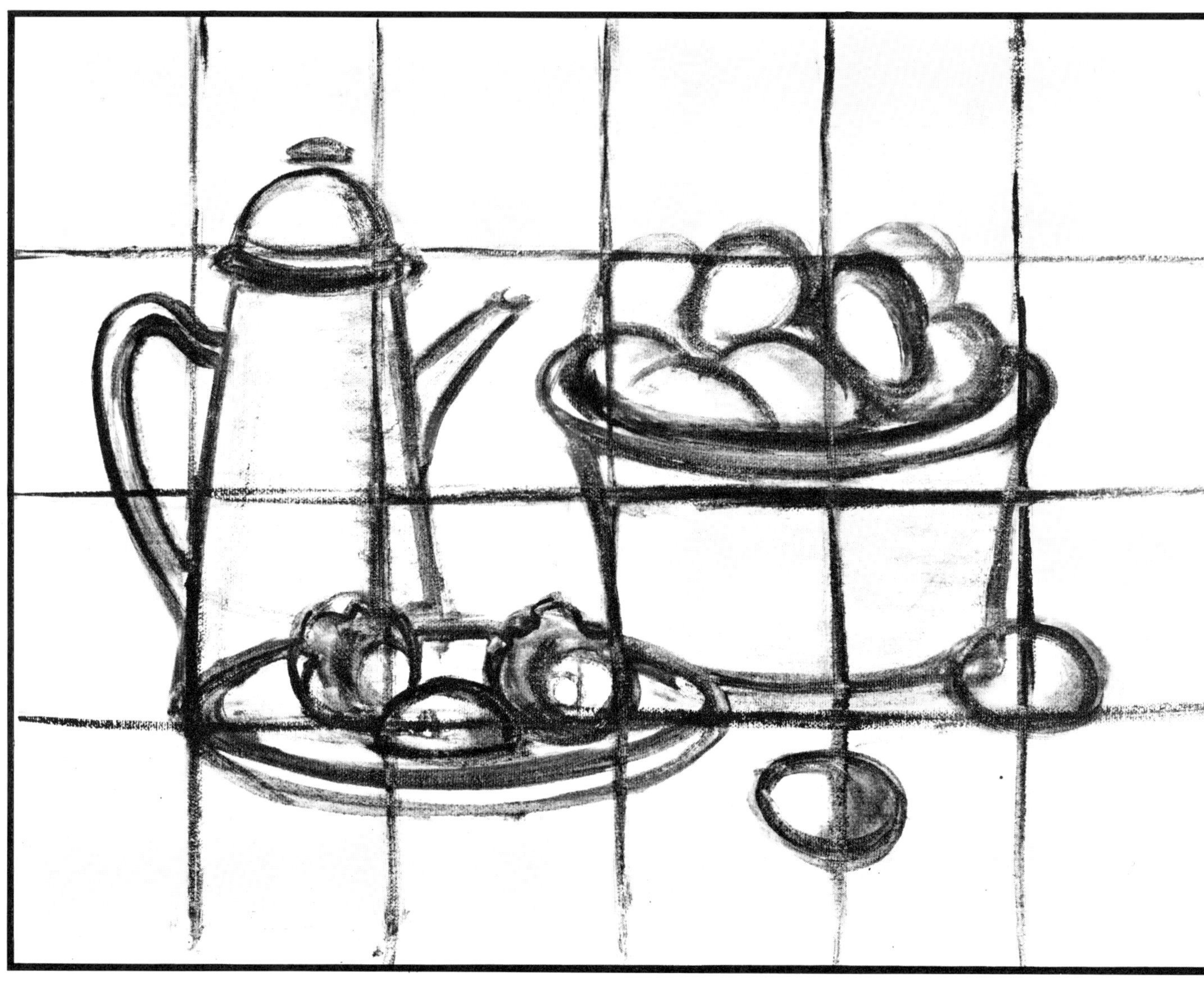

Let's paint
Use offset knife, held lightly.

1 Study the painting opposite.
2 Paint dark tone on right of canvas, using long, downward strokes.
3 Paint medium tone in the middle and light tone on left of canvas.
4 Using flat of knife paint downward strokes of purple under objects, for shadows. Add
  a little orange, then score this area horizontally with clean knife.
5 Paint a few strokes of purple, orange and aqua into background where indicated.

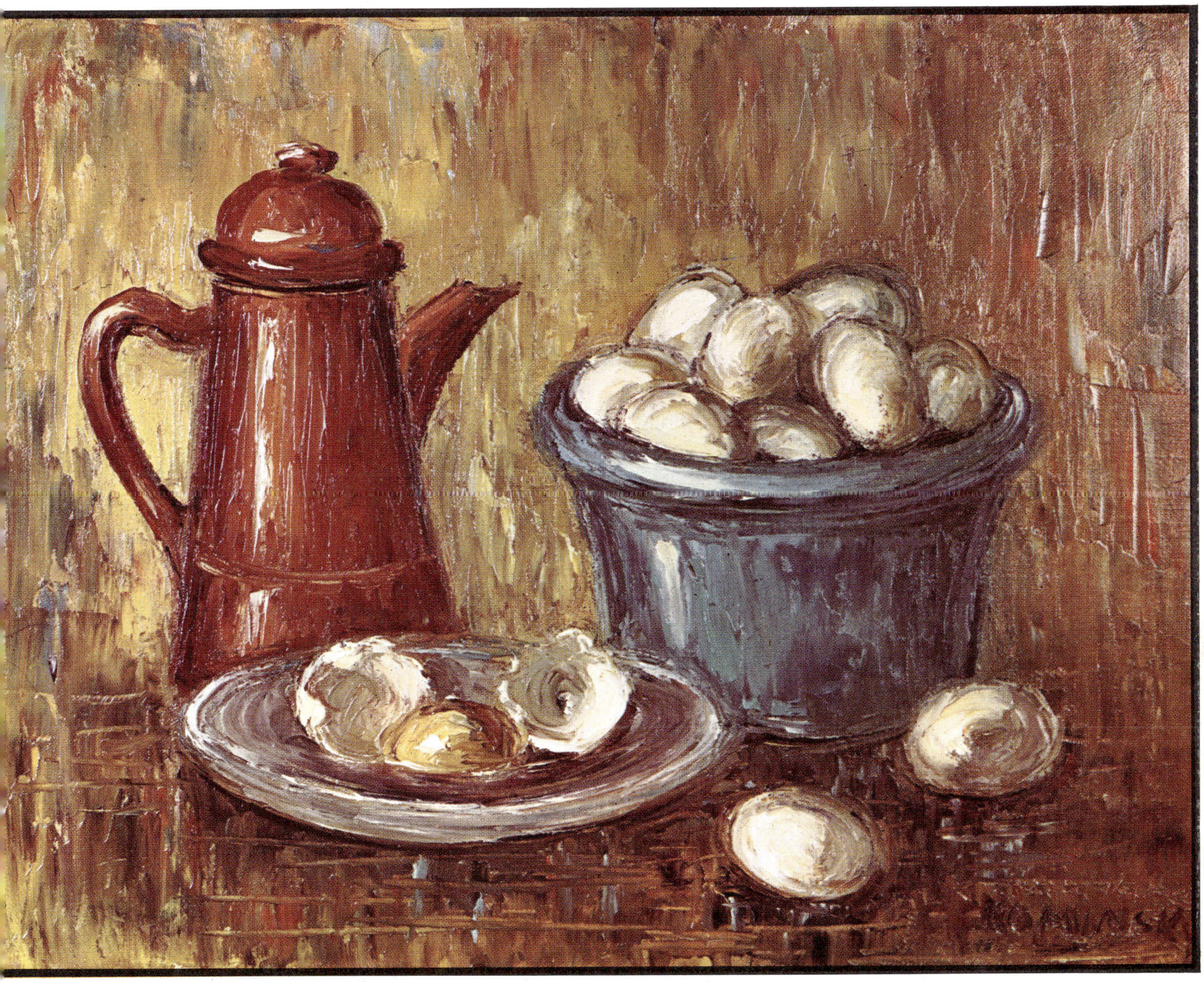

COFFEE POT

**Colour formula
Tones of burnt orange**

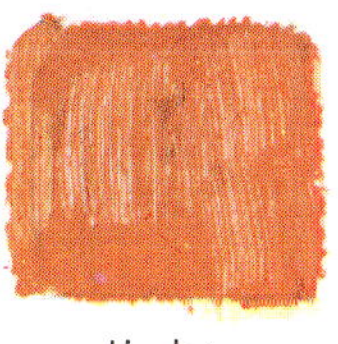 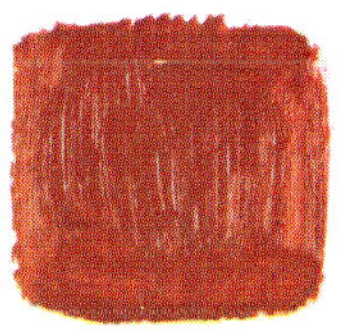 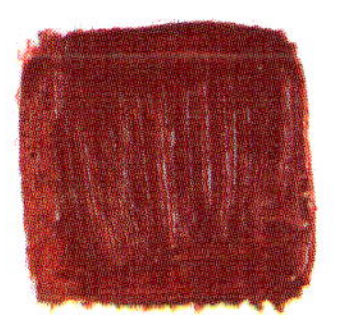

light   medium   dark

Refer to page 41 for tones of burnt orange and mix according to the directions.

1 Study the painting on the previous page.
2 Paint right side of coffee pot with dark tone. Use round strokes for the lid.
3 Paint the lip with dark tone and outline it underneath with purple.
4 Paint medium tone in the middle and light tone on the left side of pot.
5 Paint dark tone on left edge of coffee pot. Blend tones lightly.
6 Paint the spout with dark tone and a stroke of light tone above it.
7 Paint the outside of the handle with medium tone and the inside with alizarin crimson.
8 Outline the right edge of pot lightly with alizarin crimson.
9 With clean knife score a curved line across the pot near the bottom, following the shape of the lip. All highlights will be added later.

BLUE BOWL

**Colour formula
Tones of blue**

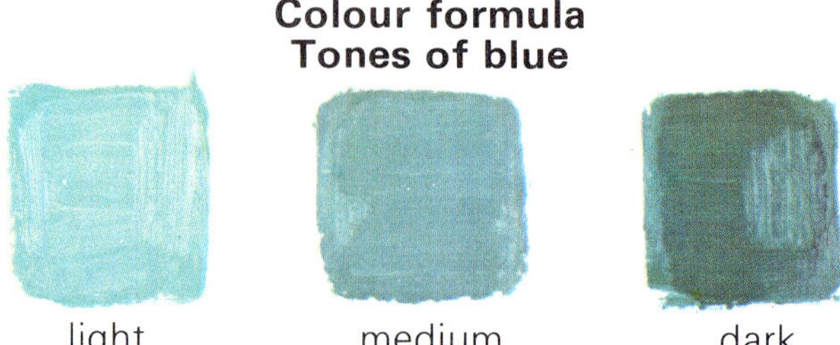

light   medium   dark

Refer to page 15 for tones of blue and mix according to the directions.

1 Study the painting on the previous page.
2 Paint dark tone on right side of bowl. Take care with the curve of the lip.
3 Paint medium tone in the middle and light tone on the left of bowl.
4 Outline under lip of bowl with dark tone and purple.
5 Outline the right side and bottom of bowl with purple.

EGGS IN BOWL AND FOREGROUND

**Colour formula
Tones of white**

light   medium   dark

Refer to page 42 for tones of white and mix according to the directions.

1 Study the painting on the previous page. Smooth forms can be a problem, so practise painting a few eggs first.
2 Paint round strokes of dark tone on right side of eggs.
3 Paint a little medium tone next, always using round strokes.
4 Paint light tone on left side of eggs.
5 Outline eggs in bowl lightly with purple.

PLATE

1 Study the painting on page 63.
2 Paint dark white tone and purple on the inside of the plate around eggs.
3 Paint underneath of plate with medium white tone and outline it with purple.
4 Add a touch of medium blue tone on the plate and coffee pot lid.

EGGS ON PLATE

1 Study the painting on page 63.
2 Paint right side of yolk with dark yellow ochre tone, using round strokes. Add a touch of cadmium orange.
3 Paint left side of yolk with yellow ochre tone.
4 Paint the two egg shells with dark white tone.
5 Paint curved strokes of light white tone on right side of both egg shells.
6 With medium round brush paint edges of cracked shells with light white tone.

HIGHLIGHTS

Colour tone
$\frac{1}{2}$ teaspoon white
$\frac{1}{4}$ teaspoon Naples yellow

1 Paint highlights down left side of coffee pot, on lid, knob and handle.
2 Paint a blob on egg yolk and a spot in centre of right egg shell.
3 Very carefully highlight round edge of plate.
4 Paint a downward stroke of highlight on left side of blue bowl and a horizontal curved stroke on lip.

With the eggs and fish, this is beginning to look like a cookery book!

Portrait of a Young Girl

PART ONE: THE PRACTICE DRAWING

1 Use canvas board, canvas or hardboard, 14 in. (36cm) by 18 in. (46cm) horizontally.
2 Study the drawings and paintings on pages 66, 67, 68 and 69.
3 Squeeze out burnt umber only on your palette.
4 Use the large, flat hog brush to stain the canvas with a light wash of burnt umber, as described in Step 1 on page 7. Wipe with toilet tissue.
5 With the medium round brush and dark umber wash put in the grid lines as indicated on page 66. You will see these are different from the usual sectioning of the canvas. With dark umber wash draw in the three egg shapes as shown.
6 Stage 1: divide the face in half (for the eyes).
7 Stage 2: a) Divide the face in quarters.
       b) Draw a short line (for the nose) dividing the lower section in half.
       c) Halfway between the nose line and the chin draw in a short line for the mouth.
       d) Draw in a line for the brows across the face, $\frac{3}{4}$ in. (2cm) above the eye line.
       e) Draw in hair line.

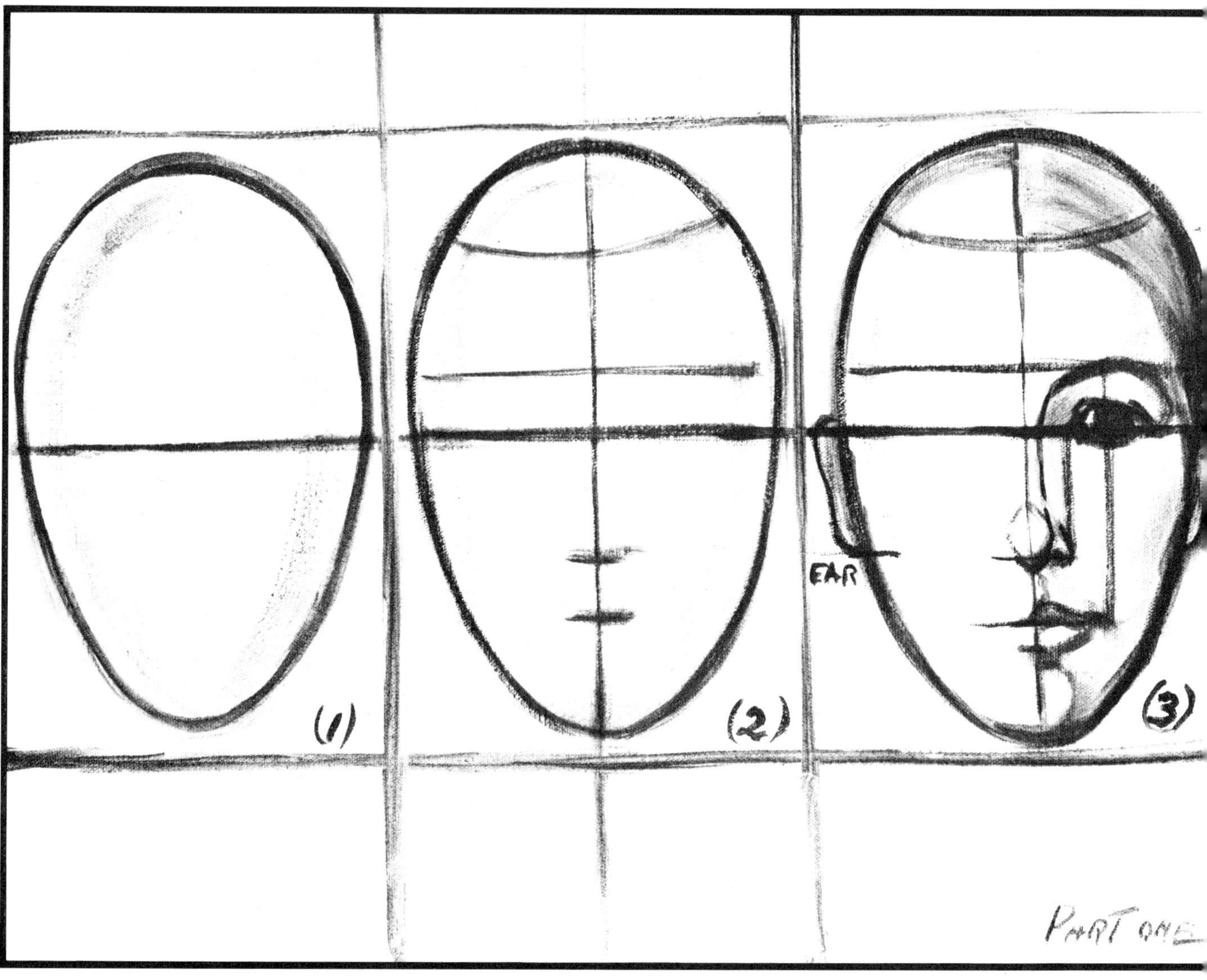

8 Stage 3: a) Draw a diamond shape for the ball of the nose, extending it a trifle below
   the line.
   b) Draw nostril as indicated (not too large).
   c) Draw in the eye, noting that the horizontal line that you drew in Stage 1
   goes through the centre. The corner of the eye lines up with the nostril.
   d) Using the centre vertical line as a guide, draw in the lips.
   e) Draw in the eyebrow, using as a guide a vertical line from brow through
   centre of eye to corner of mouth.
   f) Draw in the ears, noting that the top of the ear lines up with the eye, the
   bottom with the nostrils.
9 It is important to do this exercise a few times, so that you get the features where they
   belong.

continued on page 70

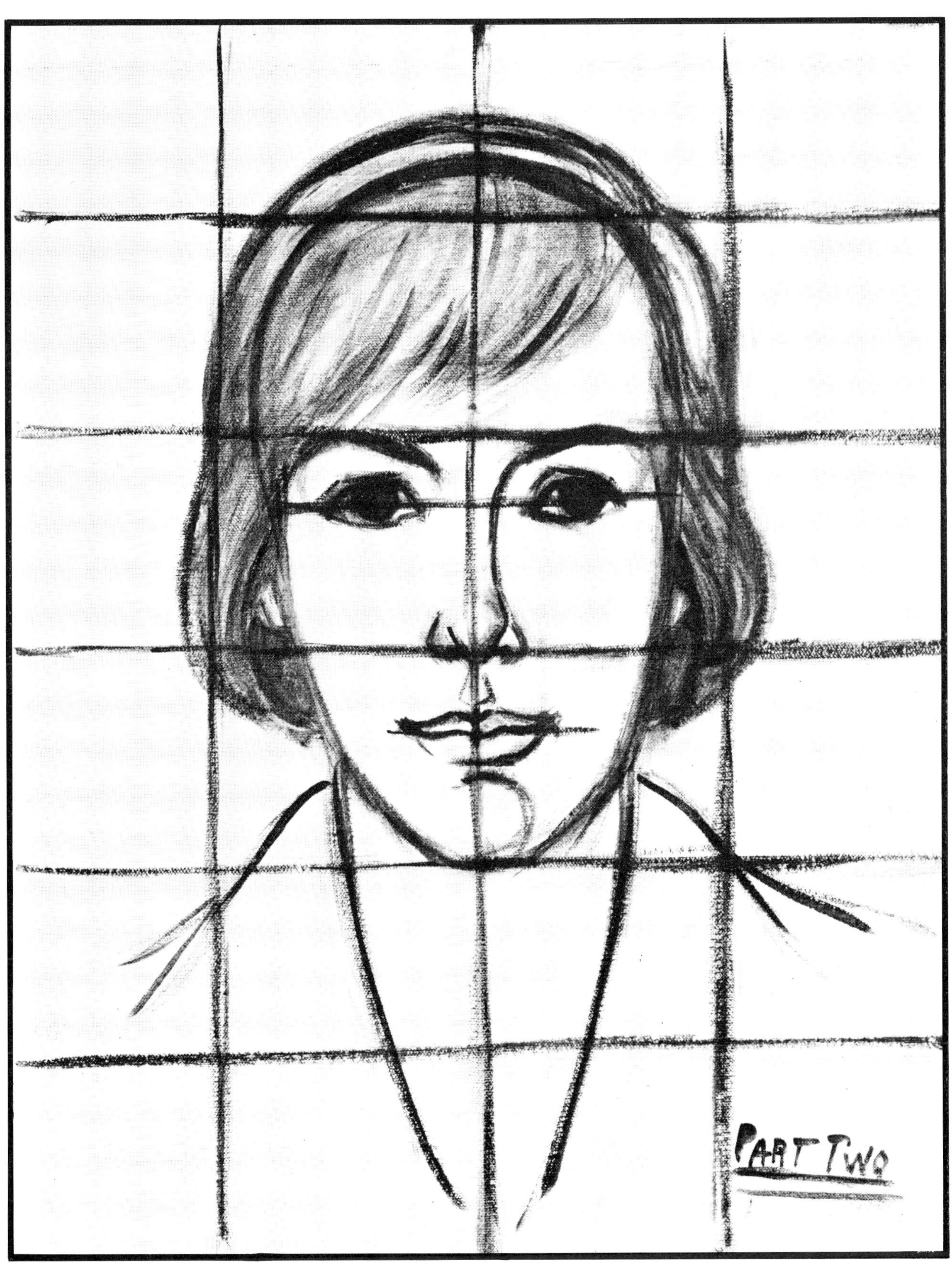

PART TWO

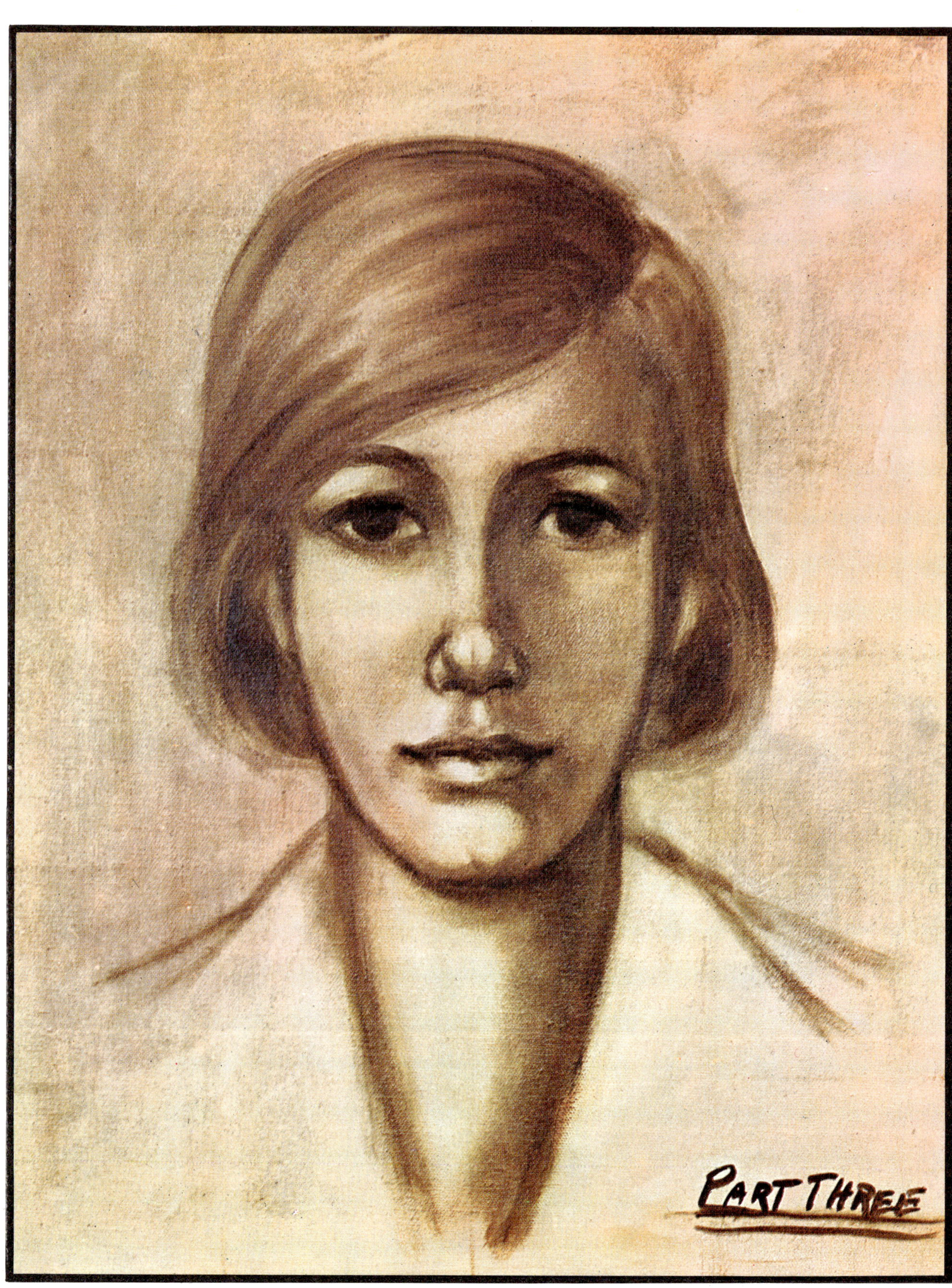
PART THREE

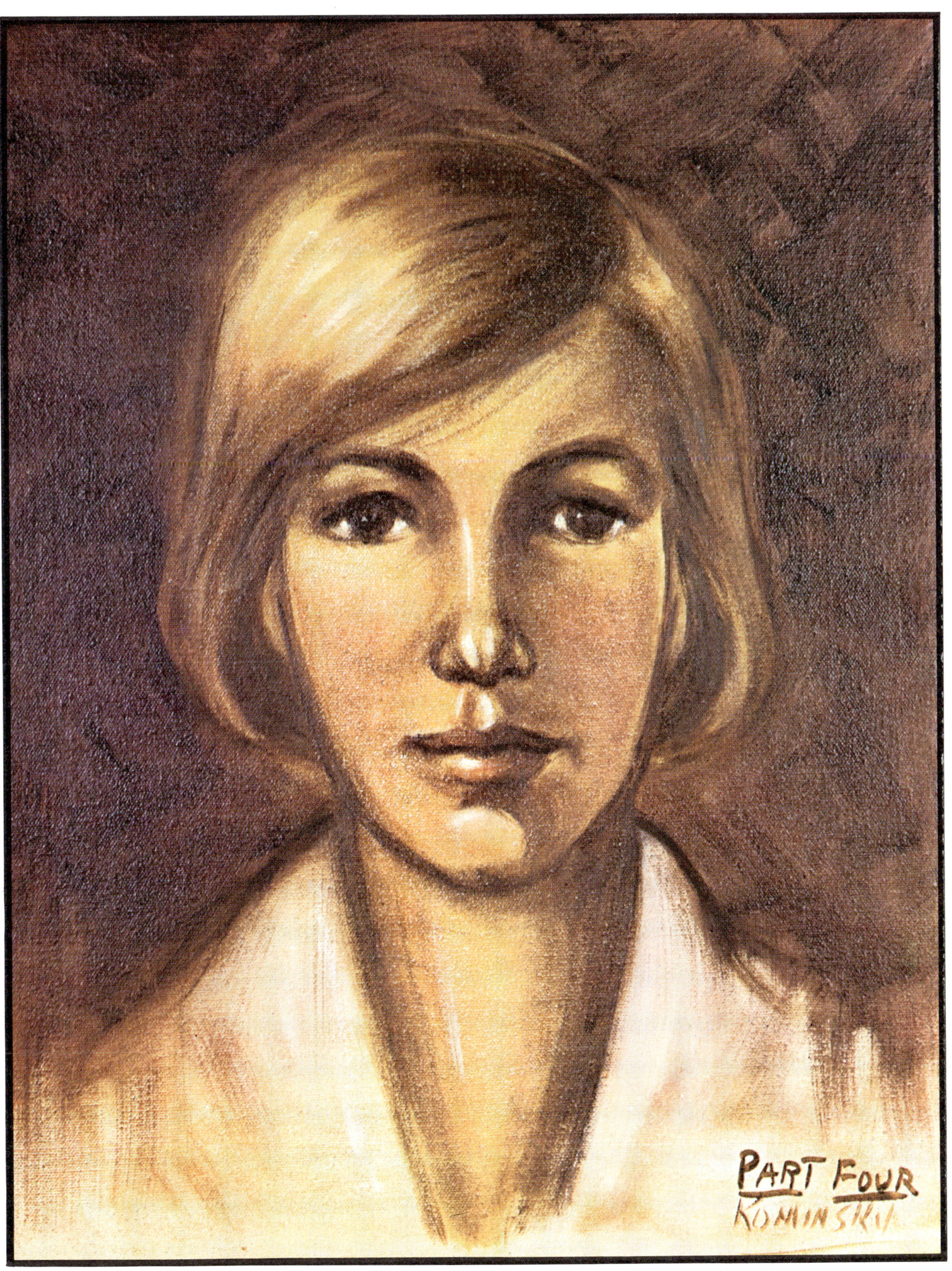

PART FOUR
KOMINSKI

PART TWO: THE DRAWING
1 Use canvas board, canvas or hardboard, 14 in. (36cm) by 18 in. (46cm) vertically.
2 Study the Part Two drawing on page 67.
3 Prepare the palette with burnt umber only.
4 Use the large, flat hog brush to stain the canvas with a light wash of burnt umber as described in Step 1 on page 7. Wipe with toilet tissue.
5 With medium round brush and dark umber wash put in the grid lines as for previous paintings. This is the usual procedure, except that this time you should keep the grid lines pale, as they will be wiped out for the final painting.
6 Draw in egg shape outline of face first. Notice that it is positioned between the fourth horizontal grid line down from the top and extends a trifle above the top horizontal grid line.
7 Draw in the features of the face, as indicated. I hope you did your homework! Be absolutely certain you have enough forehead and hair.
8 Draw in lines of the blouse as indicated.
9 When drawing is finished, or better still as you go along, wipe out carefully with tissue all grid and guide lines in face and background. Use white spirit sparingly if you must. Eliminate any white spots from erasing with a little burnt umber lightly painted on.

I suggest you now let the face dry for two or three days before shading. In this way, you won't lose the drawing.

PART THREE: SEPIA PAINTING
With the drawing dry, you can gently wipe out any mistakes you have made in the shading and not lose the drawing.

Here are some important points to note before you start painting:
Use the large, flat hog brush for larger areas.
Use the medium round brush for the more delicate areas such as eyes, mouth, nostrils and brows.
Do not rub your brush in the paint or pick up a blob — just pick up a little on the end of your brush.
The brush should be damp, not wet or dripping. Dip brush in white spirit first and dry off excess with tissue. Then pick up the paint.

SHADING THE FACE

**Colour formula
Tones of burnt umber**

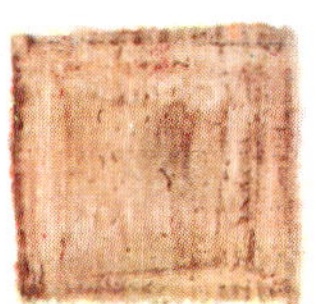 

medium   dark

Make these two tones in the same way as for the light and dark umber washes described in Steps 1 and 2 on page 7. You may have to experiment a little in order to achieve the correct tones and the correct consistency.

1 Study the Part Three painting on page 68. All recessed areas of the face are in shadow. The nose is lighter because it protrudes and catches the light. This face is in half-shadow, as the light is coming from the left.

2 Shade the right side of the face with medium tone, starting at the forehead. Watch strokes — remember, you are creating a form.
3 Shade around the eyes with medium tone.
4 Paint dark tone down the nose, from the eyebrow to the nostril.
5 With dark tone shade and soften the ball of the nose and paint in the nostrils.
6 Shade the area above the lip with medium tone.
7 Shade the area below the bottom lip and the chin with medium tone.
8 Paint the right of the top lip with dark tone, blending to medium tone on the left.
9 Paint the bottom lip with medium tone. Keep it light and soft — no hard lines.
10 The neck is always darker than the face, as the head extends out from the neck creating a dark shadow. Shade the right side of the neck with dark tone and the left side with medium tone.
11 The left side of the face is much lighter than the right, so shade it very lightly with medium tone.
12 Paint in eyebrows with dark tone, taking care not to make them too heavy.
13 Shade the eyelids with dark tone for depth — no false eyelashes please!
14 Paint eyes with burnt umber mixed with only a touch of white spirit.
15 Paint hair on left side with dark tone at the parting, shading to medium tone, then medium and dark tones around ear. On the right side, paint medium tone at the parting, shading to dark tone around the ear.

This stage must dry thoroughly before colour is applied — allow at least several days.

PART FOUR: USING COLOUR

Colour formula

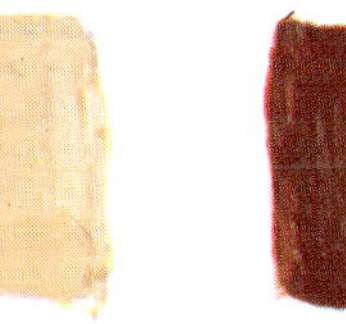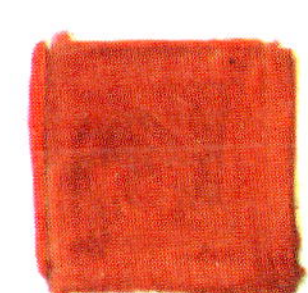

| Naples yellow | skin tone | vermilion |

The Naples yellow and vermilion are used from the palette and require no mixing. The tone for the skin is mixed in the following way:

Skin tone
$\frac{1}{4}$ teaspoon yellow ochre
$\frac{1}{8}$ teaspoon orange
touch of burnt umber
touch of alizarin crimson

1 Study the Part Four painting on page 69.
2 With clean, damp, large, flat hog brush apply a very thin coat of skin tone over hair, face and neck.
3 With toilet tissue wipe off excess skin tone, leaving an overall flesh tint.
4 Paint a little vermilion in shape of both cheeks. Wipe gently with tissue.
5 Paint a thin coat of vermilion on the lips. Paint top lip a little heavier.
6 With medium round brush paint highlights of Naples yellow on all high points of the face, catching the light on nose, area above lips, lower lip and chin.
7 Paint a little Naples yellow in the corners of the eyes for the whites. Put a tiny dot on the left of each eye.
8 Mix a little burnt umber and orange together. Paint a thin coat of this mixture in the dark areas of the hair. Highlight the light area with orange and Naples yellow.

BACKGROUND

Colour tone
½ teaspoon burnt umber
½ teaspoon purple

1 With the above colour tone paint in the background carefully, using large criss-cross
  strokes. Do not have the paint too thick.
2 With tissue blend the outline of the hair with wet background colour.
3 Drag a little background colour into the line of the blouse, to soften the line.
4 When the painting is dry, varnish it — it will lose its dull finish and look beautiful.

Now you have painted a portrait. Admittedly this portrait is based on a formula for learn-
ing purposes, i.e. composition and colour, and, in fact, we have merely tinted the drawing.
When you are more familiar with the fundamentals, you can try for a likeness. Well done!

You have just finished the paintings in this series and I'm certain you are amazed and
thrilled with the results. However, at this point you may have to learn to defend yourself.
Suddenly everyone is an art critic and you can be exposed to the 'expert opinions' of
your mate and assorted friends and relatives.

A well-meaning friend purred to one of my students on seeing her painting of carna-
tions: 'Very interesting. They are marigolds, aren't they?'

If you find yourself in a similar situation, don't be indignant or apologise. Reply
sweetly with: 'Darling, how clever! You see, it's my impression of flowers painted as if
observed from several viewpoints at once by the melting together of the various areas of
brilliant colour.' She will not understand what you are saying — and neither will you — but
she will be terribly impressed, and speechless!